FRUITFUL LIVING

YOU ARE PART OF GOD'S PLAN. YOUR GOODNESS IS WORTH IT

Scripture quotations marked (KJV) are taken from the Holy Bible King James Version.
Scripture quotations marked NKJV are taken from the New King James Version.
Scripture quotations marked CEB are taken from the Contemporary English Version.
Scripture quotations marked NIV are taken from The Holy Bible, New International Version.

....

Copyright @ 2022 by **Vanessa Boyer** All rights reserved Published by beyondthebookmedia. com All rights reserved. No part of this publication may be reproduced, distributed, or transmitted in any form or by any means, including photocopying, recording, or other electronic or mechanical methods, without the prior written permission of the publisher, except in the case of brief quotations embodied in critical reviews and certain other noncommercial uses permitted by copyright law. For permission requests, write to the publisher, addressed "Attention: Permissions Coordinator," at the address below. Limit of Liability/Disclaimer of Warranty: While the publisher and author have used their best efforts in preparing this book, they make no representations of warranties with respect to the accuracy or completeness of the contents of this book and specifically disclaim any implied warranties or merchantability or fitness for a particular purpose. No warranty may be created or extended by sales representatives or written sales materials. The advice and strategies contained herein may not be suitable for your situation. You should consult with a professional where appropriate. Neither the publisher nor author shall be liable for damages arising here from. Beyond The Book Media, LLC Alpharetta. GA www.beyondthebookmedia. com The publisher is not responsible for websites that are not owned by the publisher.
ISBN –978-1-953788-52-8 **(Printed)**

FRUITFUL LIVING

YOU ARE PART OF GOD'S PLAN. YOUR GOODNESS IS WORTH IT

Vanessa Boyer

Dedication

*I had fainted, unless I had believed to see the goodness of the
LORD in the land of the living.
Wait on the LORD: be of good courage, and he shall
strengthen thine heart: wait, I say, on the LORD.
(Psalm 27:13-14 KJV)*

I dedicate this book to my best friend, God, The Holy Spirit. Through this spiritual growth journey, I discovered exactly who I was to seek and find– the Holy Trinity. A deeper understanding of God the Father's gift of The Holy Spirit in my life released an unexplainable, immeasurable level of courage, power, and belief. I know now that everything necessary for me to have life and have it more abundantly has been provided through God's plan.

It is not me that has the power, wisdom, or confidence to control the outcomes but God, the Father, through the presence of The Holy Spirit within me. My helper is well equipped to lead me to riches untold and joy overflowing so that I might witness the goodness of the Lord in the land of the living.

This fruitful living destroys the powers of fear, worry, and doubt, which had a deep-seated hold over me. With the help of my best friend, The Holy Spirit, my faith, belief, and confidence increased and are continuously assisting me to gain victory over harmful forces. Room is being made for more of what God created for me. Greater is coming.

Thank you, best friend, The Holy Spirit

Table of Contents

Acknowledgments	9
Introduction	11
Chapter I: God's Plan	15
Chapter II: Our Help from Above-The Holy Spirit	23
Chapter III: Tightening Our Grip on Faith (Vinedresser)	27
Chapter IV: Flourishing from the Vineyard	31
Chapter V: It Starts with Love	45
Chapter VI: The Juice of Joy Overflows	47
Chapter VII: Peace is Here	57
Chapter VIII: Fertilizing the Field (Preparing to Receive)	63
Chapter IX: Rest in the Patience	65
Chapter X: Tender Touches of Kindness Matter	73
Chapter XI: Great is Thy Goodness	79
Chapter XII: Deep Rooting (Sustaining your Power)	87
Chapter XIII: Fortitude of Faithfulness	95
Chapter XIV: The Embrace of Gentleness Endures	103
Chapter XV: Surrendering to Self-Control Allows for Withstanding	111
Chapter XVI: The Blessing of Bearing (Your Inheritance)	119

Acknowledgments

There are many people whom I would like to thank for their part in helping make this book a reality. Although that number is too great to fit on this page, I want to publicly mention a few special groups and individuals for their unwavering support and encouragement.

Thank you to my friends at ElderSource who had to suffer through my lengthy Employee of the Month submissions but always encouraged me to pursue my writing.

Thank you to friends who cheered me on throughout the years and promised to purchase books as soon as I completed one. Sorry for such a long wait. Your consistent pushing kept the flame alive and made this moment possible. Mozella, you can exhale. I finally did it.

Thank you to the members of the Temple of Praise prayer line, Sister Scribes, Mornings with Abba, Sunday Sister Fellowship and Bible Study, and Marjorie Victor. Most recently, specifically during the COVID 19 pandemic and for many years before, these dynamite tribes of women have been there for me. They pushed me when I had no more push; they read, edited, prayed, sang, and joked with me all the way to this point and loved me unconditionally. I know they are forever in my corner, and I want to openly thank God for the God in them.

Thank you to my family, who shared this journey like they have shared so many times— pulling in resources, brainstorming, staying up with me during late nights, and gathering others who could enhance the process and final outcome. You define what family is to be. So glad we are all part of each other.

Thanks to my wonderful parents, Ezekiel and Maedell Boyer, who told me I could do anything. I attribute the good in my life to these two amazing and incredible people who took a chance and loved me to life. Thanks, Mom and Dad, for believing in me every second of our lives together. It made the difference. It was the difference.

And thank you to all who did a fantastic job of confirming that I have a voice worth sharing.

Blessings,

Vanessa Dari Boyer

Introduction

"But the fruit of the Spirit is Love, Joy, Peace, Patience, Kindness, Goodness, Faith, Gentleness, and Self-Control" (Galatians 5:22-23 ESV).

Thank you for trusting that the time you invest in reading this book will be enlightening and rewarding. My experiences prior to and during the writing of this book urged me to share what I was learning. I was compelled to find a way to share and expose those who thirst for a blessed and fruitful life.

Although this non-fiction book is primarily written from the perspective of believers in Jesus Christ, there are nuggets, knowledge, and examples of how any person can be equipped to change their lives, the lives of others, and the environment around them through such a relationship. We as believers know that to fully experience the gift of God, there has to be an acceptance of Jesus Christ, our savior.

I wrote this book mainly because I felt that I was missing out on the life I sought. I think many adults have moments when they ask the question, "Is this all I have to look forward to in my life? Aren't I made for more? Will my life be remembered as successful and significant?" I have been privileged to have great parents, wonderful schooling, successful career opportunities. When I would take inventory of my life, I was expecting a brighter and bolder existence. Of course, this was generated from "my" expectations.

As I mature in age, my perspectives on life change. My values change. What is essential to my fulfillment change. I often evaluate my life based on how many things I have checked off my life's to-do list. I wonder if my scorecard has more failures than successes according to the way I see my life evolving. Based on my presence in the world, will my absence be noticed?

These are just some of the thoughts that plague my mind and my memories. These thoughts sometimes lead to despair, discouragement, and, sometimes, depression. I feel they have contributed to blocking my progression in all areas of my life. I knew instinctively that this was not the life I was destined to live. Please note that I didn't include many conversations with God. Yes, there were some, but certainly not an ample amount.

Having confessed my faith in Jesus Christ over 45 years ago, I know the negative and doubtful thoughts I have are not part of God's plan for me. Jesus Christ was not sacrificed so that I could wallow in self-doubt and fear of missing out. By reexamining my life from a God-centered perspective, I grasped what kind of life God promised His children. One that He provides the means to ensure His children accomplish what He laid out for them.

Was I familiar with some of His promises? Yes, but I didn't allow them to guide my daily walk. I didn't stand in the full knowledge that God's promises were meant to inform all my choices.

When I developed a desire to know more, there was so much more to know. I am a churchgoer, bible reader, small group member, etc. But the depths of God and what He has provided for me as His child escaped me. I was afforded the opportunity and privilege to find out more about who this all-knowing, seeing, powerful being is and who He is to me.

This is a journey that will take me through eternity. That's my good news, and I want to share it with others who just might be missing the full impact God wants to have on your Christian walk and, ultimately, His creation. God's love for His children knows no bounds. As children, most of us learn the song "Jesus Loves Me". When I grew up, I confess I didn't walk in a manner that represents that I believe this as a fact in my life and not just a song.

God actually created us to soar to great heights and make a godly difference on earth. Essentially, the first commandment He specifies is for Adam and Eve to go forth, be fruitful, and multiply. He wanted them to experience productive and abundant lives, lives that demonstrate a life worth multiplying all over the earth. Why did I deny the fulfillment of such a mandate?

This book is written during the journey to disclose what seems to me as a lack of fruitfulness. A life that includes countless occasions reaching goals, just to convince myself that I cannot maintain this level of performance. See, I depended on my personal skills, overlooking that God's plan for my flourishing was wrapped up in what He supplies for my journey.

I am not a Bible scholar, minister, seminarian, or Sunday school teacher. I don't know a lot about doctrine or homiletics. I know I want to know God, Jesus, and The Holy Spirit in a way that will please them all. In a way, I can set a room on fire with zest and zeal produced by them through me, which will draw those who allow themselves to be curious out in the open.

This revelation and acceptance are driving factors in sharing this work with you. I want you to experience this truth that can move you beyond your current mindset, environment, and future. You deserve what God has specially designed exclusively for you. Dive in and get a glimpse of how this book can alter your existence as one of God's children.

This book is presented in the following order:

- God's love and His purpose for His children.
- The Holy Spirit's work and task as a conduit for believers to accomplish God's purpose.
- Faith's role in the believer accepting God's plan and His roadmap to achieving His plan.
- A mindset and environment inspiring the bearing of the Fruit of the Spirit.
- The Fruit of the Spirit–love, peace, joy, patience, kindness, goodness, faith, gentleness, and self-control.
- Everlasting benefits of The Holy Spirit's presence and the potential outcomes of obedience.

In the Fruit of the Spirit chapters, you will find the meaning of the characteristic, why it is important in God's plan, and how it produces thoughts, actions, and feelings that promote heaven on earth. These chapters include a section for reflecting. These sections provide scripture reference, reflective questions on how the characteristic shows up in your life to assist you in reflecting on that chapter, and a thought to ponder.

Throughout the book, I share some of my experiences resulting from not fully knowing God's plan to achieve my true destiny. The one He crafted for me. Also, I give biblical examples of how embracing the characteristics of the Fruit of the Spirit transformed people, situations, and the course of history.

To those who have a relationship with one, two or all three parts of the Trinity, I want to invite you to go deeper. See how God has perfectly planned for His children to work in tandem to bring Heaven to earth, specifically through the work of the Fruit of the Spirit. Our Father has given us the most excellent helper, in the personality of The Holy Spirit, to direct our efforts in walking out His nature among those who share our space. We can be the God they see, touch and smell. The Holy Spirit is there to assure we represent well.

The excitement that has overwhelmed me from a deeper revelation of God's plan for His children is something I cannot keep to myself. As a connector and communicator, I am compelled to share this wonder with all that will listen or read. I guarantee that wherever you find yourself on the spectrum in your knowledge of God, Jesus, and The Holy Spirit, you will learn that there is more to be known, experienced, and shared about what God has planned for you. I invite you to join me and see what is waiting for you.

Chapter 1

God's Plan

"But the fruit of the Spirit is Love, Joy, Peace, Patience, Kindness, Goodness, Faith, Gentleness, and Self-Control" (Galatians 5:22-23 ESV).

"When the purpose of a thing is unknown, abuse is inevitable." – Myles Munroe. This statement can pertain to animate or inanimate objects. To exist without knowing why you were created is to always be in a state of wonder — not fully certain if you have reached the mark or have tapped out your potential.

This will undoubtedly be the result if a person does not know why they were born. The person could seek growth, excitement, maturity, and validation from all the wrong sources if they are unaware of their Creator's purpose. Many years can pass, and a long life of misdirected activities can result in a missed opportunity to fully develop into the prime specimen intricately tooled by the Creator. All the good, wealth and accolades will not measure up to the ultimate intention.

Thankfully for believers, those who have confessed that Jesus Christ is their Savior and Lord, although powerful and true, the words from Myles Munroe do not describe your testimony. In creating you, God, Our Father, knew exactly what He purposed for each believer. In Jeremiah 1:5 (KJV), it says, "Before I formed, thee in the belly I knew thee; and before thou canest forth out of the womb I sanctified thee and I ordained thee a prophet unto the nations." He took great effort in crafting just the right mixture of physical attributes, talents, skills, and personality just for you. God has called you, His workmanship. What He has planned for you to accomplish in your life will set the world on fire. It will be unique and individual for every believer, and it will leave a pair of unique fingerprints on humanity.

Why was there such care and intricacy in His development of man? Why is the mold from each man and woman broken as soon as they are born? Why can hundreds of people seeing the same object see hundreds of different things at the same time? It's because He made sure that our actions, achievements, and experiences could bring glory to Him. God created each of us to love us and to be loved by us. He wanted all His children to experience an unconditional love that would keep one longing to adore the giver of love. Our actions are to glorify God.

This gift of life which God bestowed on us through breathing life into Adam is so magnificent. The mind of the wisest person could not come near to comprehending its true value. With just a short but powerful breath into the nostrils of Adam, the impossible became possible, and destinies were created. God released the power of life that could be defined by abundance. He supplied every need and desire Adam and Eve could ever want. And with that, He commanded them to "be fruitful and multiply, and fill the earth and subdue it and have dominion over the fish of the sea and over the birds of the heavens and every living thing that moves on the earth" (Genesis 1:28, ESV). Those were the first orders. This was the first mission statement created. In these instructions lay the manifestation of God's plan for His creation.

Unfortunately, Adam and Eve did not follow the original plan God had set forth for man. Disobedience reared its ugly head in the form of sin and what was meant to be a forever paradise was no more. Because of His nature, God could not exist in the midst of such darkness and brokenness. He had to display His justice towards Adam and Eve and banished them from Eden. Their lives would change forever, and because of their actions, every man born from that point came into the world with the penalty of sin. Due to the fall of man, God, the omniscient, omnipotent, and omnipresent force that He is, instituted a plan. A plan of reconciliation to bring man back into right standing with Him so that we could continue having fellowship with Him. After all, man was created for God to love him, but God cannot exist in the presence of sin and, therefore, would have been forced to abandon the very thing He loved so much–man. The fulfillment of the plan of salvation was the only way through which man could regain his desired place with God.

God sent His son, Jesus, to earth to redeem man who was lost in his sin. It would take Jesus being crucified on the cross for the sins of the world in order to bring man back into right standing with God. To suffer such a loss to save mankind, who had already demonstrated he could not or would not devote an equally committed love to God, was an example of true love and sacrifice. It was, and always will be, the ultimate sacrifice. This is how much God loves us and wants to give us the privilege to do the good works He designed for us–long before we were conceived as a possibility. He wants His children to be fruitful and multiply – to be productive, increasing in number, and doing it all to His glory.

The possibilities originating from the capabilities associated with the degree of fruitfulness God placed in man are unimaginable. God didn't intend for us to completely comprehend the vastness of what He had provided but simply accept it. We should be obedient to follow the commands and instructions to attain the blessing of abundance. This obedience comes from trusting that our Creator had everything taken care of when He created us, commanding us to be fruitful and multiply. The enormity of what God provided to man to be able to accomplish His purpose is evident in all areas of man's existence. It's seen in our thoughts, imagination, and capacity to embrace and withstand life's happenings. Also, in the actual desire we have to receive His inheritance and offer to others what they might be missing. This behavior from believers can increase the potential of people accepting Jesus and giving God glory.

God left no stone unturned, no area unaccounted for when planning and developing the amazing power He equipped man with to fulfill His original command. It would take a great amount of strength to accomplish this in the world man existed in after the fall of Eden. The level of abundant living that God foresaw for His children was much higher than the acquisition of houses, cars, boats, clothes, corner offices, etc. God foresaw the equipping of His children, enabling them to bring heaven on earth as a witness to the presence, power, and promises of an Almighty God, whose love for His children literally knows no bounds.

Before we go further, let's stop and grasp the enormity of God's love for each of His children. The best description of God's love can be found using the definition of agape love. Agape is a Greek word referring to a sacrificial love that voluntarily suffers inconvenience, discomfort, and even death for the benefit of another without expecting anything in return. God made us in His own image and expects us to mature to imitate His character. Two adjectives which highlight the intensity of this kind of love are unconditional and sacrificial. For many of us, we can't comprehend such committed action, but we must find ways to understand and embrace it.

One way God's love might be evidenced in our daily lives is by noticing small acts of His sovereignty. For example, based on something that happened at the job, you were sure you might be let go months ago for not meeting expectations. Instead, you are now up for a promotion, and you have no earthly idea how you were chosen. Or perhaps you have prayed and praised your way to humongous miracles like your mother being rushed to the emergency room with a 104 degrees fever, not expected to live through the night, but three days later, she is at the curbside waiting for you to pick her up to take her home. This kind of attention to detail and resulting miracles in the lives of His children is the product of a God who sees you as the apple of His eye. His focus is always spot on where each one of His children is concerned. He's created you in such a way that no one else in the universe is like you or will ever be like you. He has gifted you with a uniqueness that resides only in your soul. We have heard the saying, "They broke the mold when they made you." – and it's true! When creating you, God did it in such a manner that the mold was shattered the instance you stepped into existence. There would never be a need for it again, so it dissolved–never to be used again.

Like any parent, God, Our Father, wishes that no child of His suffer unnecessarily. He has put in place everything imaginable as well as those things that are not conceived in our minds that could assure safe and serene travels on this earth. We not only add to our load by not turning to Him and asking for advice — we grieve His Spirit. We ignore one of the greatest aspects of His nature, His omniscient, omnipresent, and omnipotent presence in our lives. He sees all, knows all, and is everywhere. There is nothing we could ever need that God doesn't already have available for us. We need only ask our Father.

Your understanding and acceptance of God's love and deep devotion for you will release a freedom. One that is designed to manifest the spectacular existence the Most High intended for you. In Ephesians 2:10 (ESV), it says, "For we are His workmanship, created in Christ Jesus for good works, which God prepared beforehand that we shall walk in them." You are made in perfection to be able to do the good works He has already created just for you to do. God always speaks the truth. And you can do these things—all of them. You just can't do them alone. Our society has created the façade of self-made success that endorses a philosophy that you can do it all within your own strength, power, and intelligence. Nothing could be further from the truth. God created us to live in community because He designed us to depend on Him and be interdependent on each other. He made us for one another. The self is deceiving and can be distorted in its thinking, feeling, and acting. We are fearfully and wonderfully made, but we can't fully display that wonder and awe within ourselves by ourselves. It only gets cultivated through communion with God and others. To be still and see how incredible a job God did in creating us can give us confidence in Him and His love to endure through to the end, the expected end He has for us.

You can walk in God's love and believe the vastness and presence of it in your life. Although this might sound strange, it is key to activating the level of faith, trust, and belief you will need to fulfill His purpose and have the fruitful life you were specifically designed to have.

I hope this depiction of God's love for you raises your consciousness of how much you mean to Him. You mean so much that He has entrusted His purpose on earth to you. Now that is a pretty big deal. The creator of everything has given you access to His mission–to bring Heaven on earth through you by glorifying Him. This huge responsibility would never have been placed within you had God not provided a way for your success. Celebrate the fact that God honors you with this charge. What a vote of ultimate confidence He has placed in His children. This confidence doesn't come from who we are; it comes from who is. We as believers get to be in relationship with one who doesn't just know Himself and His children but knows everything about everything. He is worthy of receiving glory.

As believers, we can confess our sins to an Almighty God. We can accept His forgiveness made possible through Jesus' crucifixion and follow His commands which allow us the potential to be fruitful and multiply to the glory of God. Now, although this sounds simple, it is anything but easy. Careful management of our mindset, which influences our actions and thoughts, is required to produce a fruitful life in God's eyes. This takes deliberate and specific activity, focus, intention, and commitment. Believers may struggle with consistently behaving in a manner pleasing to God and offering a good witness to others. It takes more than just ourselves to execute efforts towards reaching these goals. God knew this would be impossible for man. He knew it would take Himself – perfection – abiding with the believer in order to manifest the life He made possible for man to fully enjoy.

This life glorifies God and can safely secure His purposes in the center of one's life. God's purposes are used as a compass to direct His children's thoughts, feelings, and actions. Because the reality of attaining such a goal could not be achieved by man alone. In John 14:16 (KJV), Jesus said "And I will pray the Father, and he shall give you another Comforter, that he may abide with you forever." The Holy Spirit resides in each believer to give man the possibility to live out God's purpose for His creation. In the Old Testament, the possession of The Holy Spirit by the believer was not permanent in every case. The work of The Holy Spirit was seen in restraining sin and in the creation.

The believer's willingness to consider and then commit to taking God at His word and entering into a covenant designed to glorify God through fruitful living is supported by the believer's place of deep love and adoration for the one who warrants such a response–God. Catching a glimpse of being in a full-blown out embrace of His majestic love can sway a heart away from living a life that does not honor Him. One can be overwhelmed with the reality that such intense admiration and care is bestowed on them — especially in their frail, fallen human state. Yet even this incomparable force, in the personality of God's love, doesn't make the journey a piece of cake.

Chapter II

Our Help from Above- The Holy Spirit

●────────●────────●

"But the fruit of the Spirit is Love, Joy, Peace, Patience, Kindness, Goodness, Faith, Gentleness, and Self-Control" (Galatians 5:22-23 ESV).

God is all-knowing and sees the beginning and the end of all things. His plans are flawless and are made to deliver His expected end. His nature assures that if He commands a thing, He has made provisions. We are never without the appropriate resources. This also relates to His directive for us to be fruitful and multiply. God didn't leave this task up to man's finite ingenuity. He provided a surefire weapon to assist in man's journey of transforming the earth through fruitful living and multiplying efforts. The Holy Spirit, the Spirit of Jesus Christ, is provided to believers to achieve a fruitful existence through righteous living. Living that emulates what God would honor and celebrate amongst His creation.

After the work of the cross accomplished by Jesus, the Lord provided another Comforter who would be with His children forever. This gentle yet all-powerful Spirit has come to comfort and help God's children achieve God's purpose. The Holy Spirit is equal with God, the Father, and God, the Son, and is of the same essence yet distinct. The Holy Spirit has the attributes of God. He is a person who has been commissioned to take up residence in the heart of the believer. He is the vessel through which we connect to God. He is the part of the Trinity that represents the Spirit of Christ and is available to help us in all ways.

God's command to live fruitfully and multiply was to be a way of life — during times of a good harvest as well as during drought and thirst. God knew that there would be times when it would be difficult, actually impossible, to continue producing efforts that could birth fruitfulness and expansion. Nonetheless, that is what He seeks. So being the loving Father that He is, He has allowed each believer to have 24-hour access to The Holy Spirit.

When you accepted Christ, you were given the ability to produce the same evidence of God. The Holy Spirit took residence in you, and you have access to Him at all times. It is He that produces the ability in you to act out love at just the time warranted. God is not surprised by anything, and He has already created everything that will be necessary. We can walk through with His guidance. This guidance is not always accepted or sought after. Our culture can influence us to believe that we are self-sufficient and can achieve great feats without any assistance. But God specifically planned our input at the precise moment in history to create an outcome He needs to occur for the purpose He has deemed worthy. Our resistance to heeding the direction from The Holy Spirit can cause delay, denial, or destruction.

In 1 Peter 2:9 (ESV), it says, "we are called a chosen generation, a royal priesthood, a holy nation, His own special people, that you may proclaim the praises of Him who called you out of darkness into His marvelous light." So why does it seem so unrealistic to think that the things God has designed to assist in attaining abundance during our race would be out of the ordinary or foreign to the non-believer? Of course, they are nonsense to those who don't know God. But to those who profess a relationship, acceptance of such a plan should be possible. With this acceptance, we can be positioned to change the world. We are thermostats wherever we operate, and the change in an environment in just one degree can be the difference between nice and toasty and burnt to a crisp. Spiritual eyes see things that others don't. Spiritual ears hear things that others don't.

Developing this sense for how to exhibit God-like traits is a lifelong journey, and each day, there are ways to discover more. Devote time to connecting to God, who resourced you with the ability to do things you could not imagine according to the power that works in you (Ephesians 3:20 NKJV). That power is The Holy Spirit, whose sole job and purpose is to get you to be more like Christ. Become intimate with God, Jesus, and The Holy Spirit. Don't just indulge in a portion of the banquet but use each day of breath to taste parts of all of it. You can get to know what distinguishes each from the other and determine in your mind, heart, and soul what relationship you want with all three. To know the power of God, have the mind of Christ, and obey The Holy Spirit is the equation for fruitful living.

If we have a clear vision of what the expected outcome will be — pleasing God — shouldn't we be excited to execute the requirements, knowing that we shouldn't fail, especially with the helper who comes directly from God? Isn't that a no-brainer? If we keep our eyes on Jesus, pray His Word, read our Bibles, spend time with other believers and establish boundaries that reduce things not of God, we can draw closer to the life He designated for us.

The race marked out for each one is not a sprint but a marathon. It will take your entire life to experience all that is present in this journey. It is also not to be undertaken by one alone. We are in this together with others. There are other believers who are struggling just the same or, at times, worse or less than you and I. Yet, still struggling. They may be right beside you. It is no accident that we can see them, touch them, talk to them, be still with them.

Along with The Holy Spirit, they are anchors to successfully being ready, able, and willing to surrender to what The Holy Spirit deems necessary. Your heart should be right to surrender to The Holy Spirit's leading. You will need to be conscious of knowing there is an assignment chosen just for you. If our hearts are overworked, overburdened, and overlooked, we will not be in a position to effectively prepare to accept the request. It might come in many different forms —some obvious and expected, others bizarre and unimaginable. When our hearts are tender towards The Holy Spirit and God, even when there is chaos and noise all around, a tender heart can notice the urgings. It often runs ready to exhibit the fruit required for the situation. The Holy Spirit knows the duration of and needs that are appropriate for every situation. He will direct your output- the strength and the intensity. Hence a genuine awareness of the presence of The Holy Spirit and a willingness can assist in achieving a life that displays God's plan and purpose.

Chapter III

Tightening Our Grip on Faith (Vinedresser)

"But the fruit of the Spirit is Love, Joy, Peace, Patience, Kindness, Goodness, Faith, Gentleness, and Self-Control" (Galatians 5:22-23 ESV).

Knowing that we have access to the nature of God through The Holy Spirit and have the power to achieve great and mighty works is one of the most significant discoveries for a believer. One might say it could almost seem unbelievable. For many, the awesomeness is overwhelming and can lead to doubting this power that has been given by God. For this very reason, we must continue to build our faith. Faith building is part of the activity needed to prepare our readiness to handle our assignments given by God and assisted by The Holy Spirit.

What do you do to build your faith? Well, the Bible tells us that faith comes by hearing, and hearing through the word of God (Romans 10:17 ESV). You must use the Bible as your lifeline to God's precious promises and His sustaining power. It doesn't matter if you don't understand every sentence in the Bible, just show up, and God will reveal to you life-altering insights. He will give you understanding and wisdom if you ask for it. A desire is needed for being able to be fully engaged and impact situations. Wisdom is a gift freely given to all those who ask. Don't be afraid to stop in your tracks and call on God for clarity and wisdom regarding a circumstance that has you stumped. It is so much better than always depending on your own ability to discover solutions or go it solo when trying to figure out how to do something new. God has made sure we have assistance. We just have to ask.

For many years, I was guilty of thinking I had to know everything. I was afraid to ask for assistance or support because I thought it made me seem weak or stupid. I can't count the number of times I struggled through situations unnecessarily because I simply didn't ask God to help me, lead me, and guide me through. He would have gladly provided His expert assistance and knowledge, and my time would have been better utilized and available for Him. Instead, I suffered through and encountered a variety of situations over the years. Some still have negative residual effects in my life. These scars and experiences result from me choosing not to lean and depend on God, who has clearly stated and shown me that He was here for me in any and every situation. However, I prided myself on having to know it all and not requesting help. And there was always plenty of willing assistance available. People seemed to think I was "perfect," and I would prove them right. So misguided.

Why did I think I was equipped to do it alone? Mainly because my consciousness of the power and the purpose of The Holy Spirit was not at the level it needed to be in order to accept the greatest gift I ever received. I first had to build my faith in the almighty God so that I could know His nature, purpose, plan, and providence. There are specific things we can do to increase this faith, such as prayer, Bible reading, meditating on the Word, creating relationships with believers, discussing issues based on a Biblical standpoint, and numerous other actions. As I began to take these actions seriously, not relegating them to a sometimes status, I saw a difference in how I saw myself and God. And it was more important how He sees me.

Like with everything else, you will get out of something what you are willing to put in. Most of us start off with a certain level of commitment, and as time passes, the honoring of that commitment wanes. We lessen our involvement or simply cease the things we know bring us success and build our faith.

Often, I have committed to making a sacred place in my life for prayer, reading my Bible, and spending time with God. It would start great, and it was all I could talk about. And, through these actions, I was getting closer to God. I saw the move of His hand in my life and the lives of others. I was releasing my need to control all aspects of my environment and future and was comfortable asking my Father what He thought and what He wanted to see done in my life and with others.

As the story so frequently goes, when something starts working for us, we tend to make the mistake of not protecting its place in our priorities. We allow other things or people to hinder our continued embrace of that thing. How could we do this? We know we have seen and experienced positive results with the addition of prayer, Bible reading, and spending time with God. It can't be denied. However, some kind of way we loosen the grip and slowly but surely, we find these activities missing in our daily routines. I've been there many times.

We often get to the place where we think we can continue without these practices and receive the same effects that were happening when they were a huge part of our lives. It might seem like things are flowing smoothly and we are now sufficient enough to carry the load of existing in this world without these habits. But the day comes when it can be painfully obvious that we have misled ourselves. We cannot prepare for or survive the toughness of this world without a strong faith in God. Active faith to know He has a perfect plan available for each one of us as we accept Him and His Word in all things will steady our walk. Accepting The Holy Spirit's place in God's plan to bring us to an expected end requires actively building our faith as a necessary and constant part of our spiritual victory.

There are too many distractions, schemes, and plots designed to take you off the activities of strengthening your faith to ignore the one absolute thing that can protect you from such evil. As you bring these practices back into your walk, you can learn more about God and develop a deeper relationship with Him. You can be able to see clearer His strategy to protect and reward His children. First, He provided the greatest sacrifices for those who are willing to believe — salvation through the crucifixion, resurrection, and ascension of Jesus Christ. Then through sending The Holy Spirit to reside in the heart of the believer, He has offered the way to achieve His purpose on earth through His children. Genuine acceptance of such commitment and love can only be adequately understood and received through increased faith.

Chapter IV

Flourishing from the Vineyard

●─────────●─────────●

"But the fruit of the Spirit is Love, Joy, Peace, Patience, Kindness, Goodness, Faith, Gentleness, and Self-Control" (Galatians 5:22-23, ESV).

To have access to the finest and then have an opportunity for that to be elevated to an even higher level of grandeur may seem unimaginable. But with God, all things are possible. The ability to foster increase, constant growth, enjoyment, and capacity while sharing those things that one has been given is marvelous. God created the world with everything believers would need. Much of it was in the form of a seed — the object of the seed serves as the example to follow. The seed has the job of reproducing its kind, and then more of it will be present to do the same. This allows for continuous production and sustainability. Humans, animals, and plants can function in the capacity envisioned by God to accomplish what is necessary to build, sustain, and thrive. They can bring abundance out of the present reality, causing more to come into existence and continue the cycle.

God has a great plan for His children and the earth. He sees harmony present and communion carried out. To achieve this, it takes immeasurable strength, focus, and courage. However, He provided access to these forces through The Holy Spirit. Someone available with guidance, instruction, protection, and compassion for each step taken on the journey of the believer. Experiencing a less stressful and worried existence is the aim of God for His children. This can only occur when we truly give our concerns to Him. God is the one we were created to depend on — not ourselves. He is actually the solution for every situation that could ever arise in our lives. No other source has what is needed to achieve the best outcome every time. Now that doesn't mean we don't need to develop our thinking and problem-solving skills. We are to acquire knowledge, develop our intelligence, and expand our understanding to broad categories. We are to explore our potential and bring innovative and new ideas, strategies, and experiences to our world. However, the solution to all issues resides in the practice of seeking God first. Not last. We are to go to Him at the onset of our day, the close of our night, and commune with Him through the day about what we face and what we desire.

Communicating with the Knower of all can instill confidence in your value, worth and also assures you that truth is available to you. God is the source of all truth. The Bible says with this Word, God created all things. Nothing was made without the Word. Everything that was created received its life from him, and his life gave light to everyone (John 1:3-4 ESV). He knows all things, and we can trust that His direction is as solid as a rock. The answers we receive from God about how to live our lives and execute His purpose, although truthful, will not always be pain-free. We will have to fight through some situations to attain the expected end. Sometimes that fighting is going to be with ourselves. We will not always agree with or want to comply with the answers coming from God, but He has armed us with our Helper and Comforter, The Holy Spirit, to get us through these difficult times. He is also there to help us realize the beauty and grace in peaceful and joyful times. Whenever our response lines up with His plan, We can allow the purpose of God to be realized on the earth through our agreement. By demonstrating the character of Christ, believers can have victory against the plots, schemes, attitudes, feelings, and fears presented by the world. This can only be achieved by The Holy Spirit empowering the believer to bear the fruit of the Spirit. The believer is the vessel; God is the source through The Holy Spirit residing within the believer. Because of this, the believer can not only be equipped to overcome and subdue threats but to enjoy and relish all the things God's wonderment has provided for His children.

Galatians 5:22-23 (KJV)states, "But the fruit of the Spirit is love, joy, peace, patience, kindness, goodness, faith, gentleness, and temperance." These characteristics result from the work of The Holy Spirit in our lives manifesting in the believer bearing such nature in his walk. Being guided by the fruit of the Spirit allows the believer's thoughts, feelings, and actions to represent the greatest example, Jesus Christ. He displayed all these traits as He walked the earth and accomplished the Father's business. As Jesus was able to do, believers can serve as thermostats in their environment. Their yielding to The Holy Spirit to exhibit the presence of the fruit of the Spirit can set the tone and temperature wherever they find themselves. Having the mind of Christ can propel the believer to approach a situation exemplifying the nature of God, therefore increasing the probability of an outcome more pleasing to the Father (falling in line with His perfect will).

The richness of purity, holiness, and exaltation in the fruit represents a level of power and influence that believers can possess on a limitless scale through The Holy Spirit. These come directly from God, and He is infinite in all of His ways. He freely gives them to those who seek and allow The Holy Spirit to guide them. Throughout the Bible, God portrays how Jesus' use of the fruit of the spirit changed people, thoughts, and circumstances. The impossible became possible, witnessed by one to thousands. God's word painted pictures of mighty works done by demonstrating selfless behavior characterized by the fruit of the Spirit. Through studying His word, increasing their faith and belief, His children can accept and own their rightful ability to do the same. Adopting such behavior and mindset, believers can make a substantive impact daily.

Seeing such power is always better than just reading about it. God never removed it from the earth. He still empowers His children to accomplish His purpose through embodying His nature. You showing up ready, willing, and able to offer such responses can foster positive and potent outcomes and bring harmony to our communion, taking one more step towards our living on one accord.

The manner in which these characteristics are experienced can be common expressions of their nature or can be one time, never seen before demonstrations of miracles. The possibilities are enormous. The purpose is singular. God is always showing His love for His children, and His desire is for them to love Him and love each other. If it takes a miracle in a person's life for them to believe in the power of God, then expect one. Something never conceived but showing up in an expression of love, joy, peace, patience, kindness, goodness, faithfulness, gentleness, or self-control. All believers can exhibit these characteristics because they are graced with The Holy Spirit as a permanent resident in God's ultimate plan.

How satisfying is it to recognize the effects of showing up all dressed up in the fruit of the Spirit and actually controlling your environment for God's purpose? Imagine the surprise of some people when they see what power this force can have over you, especially when the behavior you exhibit is contrary to what they have witnessed in times past. Imagine how this can touch and heal forces that are binding people deep in their souls. Just the presence of kindness is capable of changing the mind of a person who is literally planning to carry out the act of suicide once they are out of your sight. Knowing someone loves you so much that they have made it possible for you to have such influence and power over their creation demonstrates enormous love and adoration. This is exactly what God possesses for each of His children. He wants the best for you and has provided a way for you to have it and for you to give it.

Chapter V

It Starts with Love

"But the fruit of the Spirit is Love, Joy, Peace, Patience, Kindness, Goodness, Faith, Gentleness, and Self-Control" (Galatians 5:22-23 ESV)

So more about this precious and powerful gift, the fruit of the Spirit. As shared previously, there are nine traits of the fruit of the Spirit. They are love, joy, peace, patience, kindness, goodness, faithfulness, gentleness, and self-control. If you haven't realized it yet, these are vital to achieving a fruitful life worthy of multiplying. God gave us the panacea to help accomplish His purpose on earth by letting this fruit bear witness in all our thoughts, feelings, and actions prompted and guided by The Holy Spirit.

We will start at the beginning with love because God is love (1 John 4: 16 KJV). The most significant act of love was displayed by God, Our Father, when He sacrificed His only begotten son, Jesus, to provide salvation for us, His children (John 3:16 KJV). That we might have fellowship with Him and walk in His light. It will take continuous study, prayer, meditation, time with God, and communication with other believers to even come close to understanding or grasping what the love of God for His children actually means. We can spend our lifetimes discovering and receiving insights on how great an act God performed just to be able to love us. God's Word is the main resource to help uncover these insights and epiphanies.

A great practical description of love is found in 1 Corinthians 13:4-7 (KJV), "Love is patient, love is kind. It does not envy, it does not boast, it is not proud. It does not dishonor others, it is not self-seeking, it is not easily angered, it keeps no record of wrongs. Love does not delight in evil but rejoices with the truth. It always protects, always trusts, always hopes, always perseveres." There are so many ways we can choose to show love, and each one is important. As humans, we might look at this portrayal of love and say, "that is simply too hard to achieve." You are right. It is impossible in our own strength. However, to possess this characteristic is the foundation for achieving God's purpose and living a fruitful life. That is why The Holy Spirit has taken occupancy in the body of the believer. He will work in the believer to manifest these traits.

As we delve deeper, keep in mind that we are focusing on God's desires for all of His children, individually and collectively. It's God's intention that we create fruitful living among those who inhabit the earth with us. It's not a solo walk but one that is filled with every kind of personality, background, experience, trauma, miracle, etc., that you can imagine.

The large majority of people on earth are constantly functioning with a "solo" view or one that only extends to their immediate family and social circles. Because of our nature and pride, it's usually a second thought and sometimes a distant second, for most, that we need to concern ourselves with the issues of others. So, it takes a powerful and incorruptible force to guide our thoughts, feelings, and actions to a communal sphere. That's what love does.

Love encapsulates everything beneficial and necessary for existence. It is the very reason why we were created. The love of God manifested in the creation of man, and the selfless determination of God that man would be preserved at all cost led to the greatest act of love. His priority was to save those He created and those who were created to love Him. God spared no expense to accomplish man's reconciliation, thus allowing the sinner to become the saint. He did not change His mind at the possibility of losing His "everything" in the process, His son, Jesus Christ. There is nothing greater than this love, and although we will never be able to completely replicate God's divine love, He has graced us with ways to love in the earth through The Holy Spirit and the characteristics of love. There is magnificent power in love.

Love calms all fears. It dries all tears. It stops undesirable behavior. It makes for the biggest smile. It mends the brokenhearted. It sets the captives free. There is no foundation stronger, more able to last through all sorts of conditions. Love is both a verb and a noun. You can show love, and you can also be loving. The way you present yourself to others and react to certain situations can be a witness to whether you are operating in love or not. One word can be a surefire testament that you are full of it or that it is so far from you that it is a source of wonder how you continue to progress day by day. With love, you have the power to touch the hearts and minds of a world of people living by their own agenda, concerning themselves with no one but themselves and those they consider family. If they are not exposed to what love is and can be, their lives may not live out the vision God has regarding the preferred state of His creation. To this end, you are on assignment. God loved you so much that He equipped you with the authority and ability to represent His love wherever you go.

Everything was created out of love and functions best when it both gives and receives love. People cherish experiences because they represent or demonstrate a loving atmosphere or a spirit of belonging, attention, or admiration. The world was created to function out of love, and therefore, without it, there is limited representation of the true vision God foresaw or very limited quantities. You can't expect to achieve the ultimate outcome if you are missing essential pieces. So, without love, nothing works the way it was designed. Love is like oxygen. When deprived of oxygen, the brain is hampered in its ability to execute all its required tasks to its design specifications. As intricately as the brain is created, the slightest irregularity can affect the expected, anticipated response. Imagine the outcomes which could result when major parts of the brain are absent. There is no telling how a person would behave. Just like our brains are designed to function to their full capacity with all the necessary parts in place, we as humanity need all our elements in place as well. Love is definitely top of this list. The presence of love secures a higher probability of positive and beneficial outcomes in all encounters.

Living in a communal space, we always involve others as we live our lives. Sometimes it doesn't seem like that is the case, but it is always the reality. Getting to an agreeable and preferred space with seven billion people on one round ball, there had to be a mechanism designed to support the existence of cooperation among this multitude. It is the expression of love among each other. When living through the lens of love, people have the ability to stop fear, blind rage, expel anger, quiet anxiety, reign over depression. They can also sense the warmth of sunshine on their arm, hum their favorite nursery rhyme, kiss their mom one more time. The list goes on and on. This is the potency of love. Achieving harmonious living embraces love and expresses it.

The heart is the controller of man's actions, and however it develops will determine man's thoughts, feelings, and behavior. Exposure to those things that are not loving, caring, or protective will develop cold, sterile, and distant attitudes that cater to selfishness, greed, and bitterness. Those who find themselves without symbols, signs, and expressions of love will fill their minds with ways to please their own appetites, often at the expense of others. They have not experienced the value and benefit of being the recipient of a heart that seeks to find those in want, calms broken spirits, laughs at ridiculous jokes, weeps at lost opportunities experienced by others, and follows where The Holy Spirit leads.

You have been given this privilege to influence the direction of hearts and souls of those God connects to you. Showing thoughtful concern is a good example of how to express love. Doing or saying something positive for the express benefit of another person is a loving gesture and is so needed. You "come out of you" and focus on another. Now that can be fairly common for most people when the situation is agreeable. An example is when something has happened with or to another person, and there is a clear sense of need. People involved want to help and move the situation to an acceptable end. In this instance, everyone is comfortable with what has taken place with the situation and just wants to be helpful. However, what happens when conflict arises, and there is no clear response to yield a favorable outcome? What is a person to do? Follow their nature? Retaliate? Would such action bring about the harmonious environment God desires? Most likely not. It is a harmony that encourages fruitful living.

In circumstances where the expected action is not going to bring order or peace, love must intervene. Love must show up and battle the negative forces trying to rob the peace and illicit prideful responses. It must go contrary to what is in a man's heart by his own nature. Love inspires one to be the bigger person and turn the other cheek. This is not easy. It's actually impossible without help. Remember, your helper, The Holy Spirit, is right in the midst of the situation with you. He is aware of the end from the beginning and knows exactly what is needed. He also knows assuredly that you can deliver because He is there to guarantee it if you allow Him. The Holy Spirit has been given to each believer to drastically increase the probability of them landing at the exact spot designed by God during their journey. Their stumbling blocks that may be encountered will not be so detrimental that they will not prevent the believer from regaining course and direction. You will always have the opportunity and the ability to resume the course that leads to that expected end.

With the trials of the world and the numerous missteps we all make, there has to be visible evidence or things that produce emotional and physical awareness that the power afforded the believers by God is real. Something that makes one trust I will make it if I stay the course even after resuming it hundreds of times. Such visible evidence comes from encounters with believers producing the characteristics of the spirit of Christ. The fruit of his person. The fruit of the Spirit.

You, as a believer, are equipped to be suited up at all times. Your heart is tender towards God and allows you to be sensitive to things that others are often oblivious to. This tender but capable core gives you an added advantage in winning battles that you are called to fight as well as those you are called to help fight. So be not afraid; you and The Holy Spirit are well able to exert the Father's love flawlessly.

Manifestations of love come in many different ways. Silence when there is nothing to say. Just the right word when silence is too hard to bear. Glasses of cool pink lemonade on the back porch of grandma's home in the summer. A switch touching your backside more times than you care to remember to deter actions that could provoke stronger repercussions. Now, this type of love is not always well received. It is not always understood. It is not always appreciated. These reactions do not mean that love was not offered, expressed, and given. You and The Holy Spirit know your intent, and sometimes it takes several encounters for the object of your love to recognize what they are experiencing. This is one reason when it is paramount that we remember love is action. Thinking love/loving thoughts towards a person doesn't have the same effect as acting it out. The recipient doesn't get the benefit just from your thoughts. You have to display those thoughts in motion and choose recognizable and meaningful actions.

Now, there will be times when your demonstration of love will not be acknowledged, appreciated, or understood, but our directive is to commit to them – not to concern ourselves with the reactions they illicit. Yes, that can be painful, frustrating, and disheartening. Our Father knew as much; that is why He equipped us with The Holy Spirit and His word. In Joshua 1:9 (NIV) it says, "Be strong and courageous. Do not be afraid; do not be discouraged, for the Lord your God will be with you wherever you go.

We don't have to worry about not having our Father right with us, giving us the love we are trying to offer to others. The Holy Spirit has just the right amount of power to encourage you to carry out the act of love so desperately needed while being assured you will survive the reaction. Just trust and go on loving.

Remember how you felt when you felt loved. What was your reaction? How did it guide and direct your thoughts, feelings, and behavior? Was it for the good? The good of many? Could you see the long-term benefits of it? Capture those positive endorphins using your brilliant mind and heart and commit to giving back that which might cause the same kind of reaction, admiration, and comfort to others for the glory of God. We are all basically longing for the same things, and that is why it is possible for us to offer what might be needed to one another. Now, this is where the heart can play a big part. For people who are not used to seeking comfort, peace, and steadiness in others, it might be challenging for them to begin looking for and recognizing such support outside of themselves. However, it is possible. Remember, their hearts responded to the love generated from another. There is hope. The reciprocity factor can be a key determinant in our responses when receiving love. The power of love is stronger than anything created. Remember, God is love and sharing love, acting out of love, receiving love – it's all about Him.

Let love be your calling card and your strategy of choice when running your race. Keep your heart pure from hatred and strife. Remember, you are divinely designed to succeed in your duty. You are part of a bigger plan. God's purpose will be achieved, and He has equipped those who accept this challenge through salvation with supernatural assistance to gain ground and make a mark on His creation. Draw your daily strength from knowing how much God loves you. You are His special child. Wrap yourself in the adoration, protection, and exhilaration felt when you are conscious of the vastness of His love for you. This will enable you to exhibit love during those times when just the opposite is trying to rear its ugly head. You know the power, the euphoria, the whirlwind of excitement that exists when love is shown. Extend it and be the image of God people need at any given moment.

Fruitful Yield: Love

Scripture to Read:

For God so loved the world, that he gave his only begotten Son, that whosoever believeth in him should not perish, but have everlasting life (John 3:16 KJV).

Questions to Answer:

What will be your yield of love today?

Did you see love displayed today, and if so, how?

Thought to Ponder:

Be the heart of God; love like crazy!

Chapter VI

The Juice of Joy Overflows

"But the fruit of the Spirit is Love, Joy, Peace, Patience, Kindness, Goodness, Faith, Gentleness, and Self-Control"
(Galatians 5:22-23 ESV)

Love is at the foundation of every action The Holy Spirit inspires in your life. It is all about extending God's love to you as you commit to loving God and fulfilling His purpose. Out of this position, other traits flow and are catalysts for abundant living. Each trait has a unique essence which, when fully activated, is very distinctive. Joy is especially unique. It can show up in the most unexpected places and command the most amazing responses. Joy has been defined as a feeling of great pleasure and happiness, inner gladness, delight, or rejoicing. It has been said that this inner gladness can lead to a cheerful heart, and a cheerful heart can lead to cheerful behavior. One comment that might be unexpected is that the most important attribute of joy is that you can find it in adversity. Even though we have all heard that before, it's no wonder so many might find it strange. This is because we often find it difficult. Overall, it seems counter-cultural to seek joy in a bad situation. However, we know that our walk with Christ is just that, counter-cultural to what is being displayed and accepted in our societies.

Joy has elements of tenacity which allow it to be unmoved, even in the face of circumstances or temperament. When often compared to happiness, which is quite frequently associated with what is happening at that moment, describing joy in similar terms really diminishes the essence of joy. There are some prerequisites for happiness that are not deal breakers for joy. The circumstances could be far less than perfect, and joy takes a seat in the midst of the situation. The expected outcome can be gloom and doom, but it doesn't scare joy away. In fact, joy increases its intensity just to compensate for the less-than-stellar circumstances present. It can make the low high, the weak strong, the tired revived, and the sick well. Guess what? It is also contagious. Joy can leap from one soul to the another just by proximity and change the outcome of an entire situation with an indescribable explanation. Do not let the lust of the flesh, the lust of the eyes, and the pride of life burden you down so as to not let the essence of joy flow naturally and instinctively.

By its nature, joy can be found when it encounters a painful situation or broken heart, needing wholeness. In those moments, joy allows us to believe in healing, be encouraged by connection, and embrace the potential of future celebration. Believers who freely allow The Holy Spirit to work through them can become automatically sensitive when identifying or sensing a presence of heavy weight or spiritual affliction. This awareness comes from your decision to honor the gift of being designated to receive the most powerful force on earth as a dweller with and in you. The Holy Spirit will lead you to hone in on certain situations, remind you of how joy expresses itself, and help you produce just the appropriate action to address the current need. No matter how often you have created joy for others and lifted up a weary soul with your smile or touch, you will always need the power of The Holy Spirit to receive a greater yield. Inviting The Holy Spirit, the empowering agent, into every situation is the best display of wisdom.

Like God, our Father, God, The Holy Spirit knows the future and is aware of what is necessary for all circumstances. He is able to guide you such that your actions can provide a person with joy for their current and next stage of life. We don't possess this ability alone. We are the vessel for the fruit to come from and through, but we don't have access to the total big picture. Only God through The Holy Spirit has such knowledge and wisdom. Therefore, let us receive assistance in executing our assignment.

A Bible story that reflects joy from a place of deep sorrow to a mountain top cry is found in Mark 5:22-41 KJV. This passage describes the encounter with Jesus in which a prominent leader and a forgotten woman both found joy, unspeakable. Jairus, the ruler of the synagogue, knowing the power of Jesus, sought Him out to request healing for his daughter. His little one lay still in her bed at home, almost lifeless. When Jairus approached Jesus, he fell to His feet, showing honor and respect while formulating his petition for help. Agreeing to see the child, Jesus and Jairus were on their way to the ruler's home. During the journey, Jesus encountered the woman with the issue of blood. Scorned and outcast for many years, this woman also knew of Jesus' healing power. She didn't ask for much, just to touch the hem of His garment and her belief assured her that she would be healed.

Pressing her way to Jesus, the woman made contact with Him, and suddenly, the flow of blood ceased. This moment produced such a virtuous exchange of power that Jesus stopped amidst a crowd of people and asked,

"Who touched Me?" A woman who had been the target of pain, suffering, greed, ridicule, and disappointment for over twelve long years was now free of that burden. She allowed her faith to remove the issue and release the joy. As Jesus searched for the one who received His anointing, the woman stepped forth with all the courage she could muster and confessed her act. Due to this joy-produced bravery, she continues to be the only woman in the Bible Jesus refers to as daughter. (The Only Woman in the Bible, Jesus Calls Daughter by David Ettinger) Jesus looks on her and says, "Daughter, thy faith hath made thee whole, go in peace and be whole of thy plague." What a testimony to experience. The gift of God's word affords this and many more miracles to be recounted throughout eternity. No doubt this woman had perfected her faith building practice

This story reminds us of God's omnipotence. He can do all things well. The successful healing of the woman with the issue of blood did not negate the intended healing of Jairus' daughter. As they all witnessed the miracle of the woman, servants from Jairus' house met him and Jesus on the road to report that there was no need to bother Jesus any longer because the little girl was dead. Let's put ourselves in his shoes. Standing right by the Healer himself, you get the news that it is too late. Hope that existed in your approach to seek and find your answer just vanished while standing with the answer. What are you to do? There is no joy in sight. And then you hear the Master say, "Be not afraid, only believe." What is there to believe? Many witnesses have brought the news that it is simply too late. However, when the Healer of the universe says, "Wait; not yet." You believe in Him. Jesus arrives at the home of Jairus, traveling with Peter, James, and John. He dismisses the crowd bearing false witness to the truth that lies within His power. He clarifies to the audience that the little girl is not dead but just asleep.

The environment must be suitable for joy to enter. During the time Jesus walked the earth, He knew the true spirit of a thing, place, or person. He always knew what lay deep at the core. After His death, we were given The Holy Spirit to be able to identify such matters, as our savior did. At Jairus' home, Jesus only allowed those He knew had deep faith to accompany Him in the little girls' room. Peter, John, James, and the girl's family had the right level of faith for this miracle. Jesus took the hand of the child and said unto her, "Talitha cumi," which is being interpreted, "Little girl, arise" (Luke 8:54-55 NKJV). Immediately after this act, the girl, who was twelve years old, arose and walked. Amazement filled the room, and Jesus commanded the girl's parents not to speak of this miracle but to prepare food for their daughter.

Whether you are a parent or not, hearing of this feat brings rejoicing to your heart. Not long ago, Jairus' hope, which was fueled by his knowledge of Jesus, was crushed by the words of the crowd. Now through obedience to the petition of Jesus, to only believe, he was able to receive the blessing of unspeakable joy. Joy comes to those who wait and often to those who wait with bruised expectations. But with God on the scene, faith the size of a mustard seed produces a harvest full of joy.

For this reason, humility was a prerequisite for following Jesus and still is when following the leading of The Holy Spirit. We must let go of ourselves and the preconceived ideas of our power, strength, knowledge, and ability. The Holy Spirit represents the One that is all-knowing. There is nothing that tops Him, and He resides in every believer. So, don't fight it. Stop warring with your flesh. Let it rest and take up the presence and direction of The Holy Spirit. He knows this is easier said than done. He knows we stumble at times and lose face. In times like those, remember, you couldn't lose face in front of the one who truly knows you. The one who knows you better than you know yourself.

Don't be deceived by the evil one. His objective is to convince you that he knows the "real" you. He promotes the continuous dialogue of all the mistakes and lies of your past, highlighting the negative emotions that seem to characterize your entire existence, or so he wants you to believe. His ultimate goal is for you to spend 23.9 hours a day hiding these deeds from the world. He is trying to force you to accept a bold-face lie about yourself. He would have you believe that you are not a candidate for joy, much less a giver of it. Stomp his voice and spirit out. Listen to the One who truly knows you. The One who knows who you were created to be and what you were created to do because He created you for His purpose.

Believer, you must revel in your assignment to be the fountain of joy where The Holy Spirit directs. How great is it to know you have an unwavering strength that can keep you upright when the winds of the world blow so hard towards you? The world is full of unforeseen tragedies and daily drama. The ability to channel through these times as if nothing is happening can be short-lived, especially if hit by magnificent challenges. Having a force that can see you through the battle and push you back up again sustains our spiritual growth. It counteracts the cultural expectations, which would have you down for the count with no resurgence in sight. It's like the glue that can surely hold together what would under any other circumstance be torn apart. How do we reach that level of abundant living if we don't have a tool that keeps us fighting when we are losing? Something that helps us see that things might be changing for the worse, but there is still hope available through that change.

Our memories are good allies for activating joy at a deeper level. They can remind our hearts and minds that what is now was not always nor will it always be. They prompt us to acknowledge that there is comfort in knowing that change doesn't always cause permanent destruction. Remember when you came out of a situation that at its onset looked too tough to tackle? You couldn't see your way through. But through you came. You conquered the obstacle, and joy filled your soul. The joy was residing in you all the while, exposing itself to you along the path, keeping you company and committed to reaching an acceptable end. This goes a long way in proving your strength far outweighs that which you previously considered the point of no return. Our Creator knew the resilience needed to claim victory over the desires to give in and forfeit our blessings. He gave joy power to produce gladness from the most precious of times all the way to the most tragic. It shows up through the still small tickle that comes from the smell of your favorite meal by one of your favorite people. This can bring back to your mind how you are uniquely different from anyone else in the whole world. You have been given the privilege of living your life in and with this uniqueness, and that is no small feat.

Sharing is one of the best ways to extend joy. When you are full of contentment, even when things are not going the way you planned or the way that makes sense, you give evidence of the strength and power necessary to make it through. You are able to keep moving through the pain while expecting a better outcome than you see. Our attitude is the carrier of the things from our hearts, which can influence our atmosphere. An attitude that is dressed up to receive anyone who appears, no matter how they arrive, can emit acceptance and warmth. This could combat many negative thoughts, emotions, feelings, or behavior looming around. Seeing how a person with joy in their heart reacts to adversity as well as everyday routines can invite the interest of others. It can entice a change or at least stir up curiosity to have a closer look at the reason for such a response. Your big smile, gracious handshake, boisterous laugh, soft word with a hug, or just a look of tender concern can declare the presence of joy.

Joy is a game-changer in life. It comes in small, medium, and large sizes. Some of the ways joy is expressed are so subtle but timely. Here are a few examples of how joy has played full court in so many lives: Excitement from a tea party for your 108-year young girlfriend who is dressed from head to toe. Seeing the hurt in one's eyes and then relinquishing the time you had hidden away for your favorite pastime to give some time to this one who has had hardly any visitors and needs to talk. It can bring a faint smile to the face of an older widow who just lost her spouse of 75 years. A memory from times gone by surfaces in her mind as she rides home from the cemetery, which seemed to be hundreds of miles from her kitchen. It has been known to show itself through the height jumped by a 6-year-old at his first big boy party–friends and family all around and him being the main attraction. It can also be recognized when you've lost your job, and while at home looking for a document to complete an overdue application, you come across a $20 bill in the pages of a book you had no business reading at that moment. You can only smile and say thank you, Lord, aloud.

Celebrating those around you who go through days as if there is no love to receive or peace to seek is life-changing and infectious. A brilliant smile is a byproduct of the radiance of God's light inside a person filled with joy. They can't stop it from forming, and in a blink of an eye, it's a beacon drawing the downcast, forgotten, isolated souls longing to have some of that. You, as a believer, have access to this, and you can share it with others.

The Holy Spirit has empowered and prompted the believer to be on watch for the needs of the world around them. When you sense a concern that will not be addressed if you don't reach out, you can reach out and engage. What a perfect opportunity created to guide those from dark and heavy places to a point where the light of His glory shines directly on them, chasing away the heaviness and darkness. Letting it be known that there is survival around the corner and this temporary pit stop is meant only to give you the opportunity to see a force that can sustain you through to a way out. It is not easy, but it is worth it. Joy makes grief, sorrow, and disappointment more palatable. It allows for experiencing the unconditional love God created for His children. It can make the journey not just bearable but delightful, especially when you travel knowing you are just passing through. Joy is the fuel that balances the passing of time. Fill your tank until it overflows.

Fruitful Yield: Joy

Scripture to Read:

Rejoice in the Lord always: and again, I say, Rejoice (Philippians 4:4 KJV).

Questions to Answer:

What will be your yield of joy today?

Did you see joy displayed today, and if so, how?

Thought to Ponder:

Joy is here now. Move in it!

Chapter VII

Peace is Here

―――●―――――――●―――――――●―――

"But the fruit of the Spirit is Love, Joy, Peace, Patience, Kindness, Goodness, Faith, Gentleness, and Self-Control"
(Galatians 5:22-23 ESV)

Peace. Everyone is clamoring for it, but do they know what it is, and will they recognize it when they see it?

One definition says that peace is freedom from disturbance, tranquility. Inner peace is referred to as a state of being mentally and spiritually at peace with enough knowledge and understanding to keep oneself strong in the face of discord or stress.

In the Bible, John 14: 26-28 (NIV), says, *"But the Advocate, The Holy Spirit, whom the Father will send in my name, will teach you all things and will remind you of everything I have said to you. Peace I leave with you; my peace I give you. I do not give to you as the world gives. Do not let your hearts be troubled and do not be afraid."*

As with everything, the Bible has a word for all situations. This passage provides us with an assurance that Webster nor Google can capture.

Peace is an armor made of impenetrable force. If deeply rooted in the believer, very little is strong enough to shake it. It can produce a willing and able attitude to stand and confront whatever has to be faced with courage and calmness, knowing that the thing or situation will not last. It reminds you that you are not alone. Circumstance came to pass, and you can and will stand. Peace is independent of the outcome or the variables associated with the situation. It declares victory because it truly knows its essence and staying power.

Many people think that peace can only be present in the absence of pain, conflict, argument, resentment, and negative consequences. They associate peace with everything having to be perfect. This notion couldn't be further from the truth of what peace is and requires to exist. It is available every minute of the day and in every situation. It can provide great comfort or just keep you from taking that wrong step — whichever is needed. Isaiah 26:3 (KJV) states, *"Thou wilt keep him in perfect peace, whose mind is stayed on thee: because he trusteth in thee."* Concentrating on the source of our peace actually produces peace. It is like an exchange between a mentor and the protégée. The act of adoration creates an environment where what is needed can be received, showing God, we trust Him to be with us in all situations and to be the ultimate caretaker creates the environment where God can freely deposit in us what is needed. He's bigger than anything we could ever face and has had victory over it all. Remember that Jesus said that The Holy Spirit will teach us all things and remind us of everything He has said to us. We will be reminded of the victory God has already attained for the benefit of His children. Our peace is the spoils of that victory, and it is ours to freely give as well.

Peace can ensure you will be there to fight again, not in your strength but in Your Father's. It is a place of sustainability in the storms. Your walking in peace is evidence for those who come behind you to realize that this situation did not overtake the one in the midst of it. They were able to weather it and come out of it with scars that bear the marks from being in the presence of a loving God. Your resilience can light the way out of no way and give hope to the hopeless. It can allow for clearer vision and an open mind to possibilities that were thwarted due to the ravaging winds of those storms, as well as the what-ifs of the challenges faced in a day.

Peace can offer both solace and pleasure at the same time. In Romans 12:18 (KJV), the Bible tells us to live peacefully among all men, as much as we are able. Creating environments that promote support and not friction is very appealing. By deciding to pursue and promote peace, we can make this possible. This could drastically change the atmosphere of our communion with others and make people rethink their thoughts, feelings, and actions. It might also allow people to see futures they had once hoped for and never thought would be possible. You can walk in a room and speak to anyone about whatever is on your heart and mind when you have allowed peace to take up permanent residence. You don't have to run looking for it. You bring it wherever you go. It is just a prayer away. Even in the midst of uneasiness, you realize that it can be called on and will make its presence known and felt instantly. Never doubt its power — it is known to calm storms.

Being filled with peace and having it on display as part of your nature, or being available when The Holy Spirit prompts your demonstration of it, can show up in many ways. Peace might come from sipping a nice hot cup of ginger tea in your grandmother's rocking chair or packing up from a full day of fishing with your son. It could be sitting still on the edge of your bed after coming home from your last chemotherapy or kissing your loved one on the forehead while they lay in a state, ready to be seen no more. Peace provides rest for the mind and the heart. It is not the absence of trouble but the tenacity to stay still in the midst of trouble. You do not have to know what the outcome will bring but know that it all came to pass. You can be well able to conquer any mountain with your mountain slayer, God — our Father. This is the reward of peace.

The atmosphere you create will affect everyone who enters your space and the spaces you enter. The aura that is present can catapult those in the midst to take on the character of that spirit. Let it be said that those who find themselves in your presence can receive the secret aroma of calmness no matter the circumstance. Yes, there is sorrow dwelling in grief. Yet peace can still be there. This truth makes it important to realize that it is a choice of what we receive from the surroundings and atmosphere. Our choice will determine how successful we will be at living peacefully with all men.

Fruitful Yield: Peace

Scripture to Read:

The LORD bless thee, and keep thee: The LORD make his face shine upon thee, and be gracious unto thee: The LORD lift up his countenance upon thee, and give thee peace (Numbers 6:24-26 KJV).

Questions to Answer:

What will be your yield of peace today?

Did you see peace displayed today, and if so, how?

Thought to Ponder:

Peace has lifted the mist cast by uncertainty and declared survival... Victory is ahead.

Chapter VIII

Fertilizing the Field
(Preparing to Receive)

•———————•———————•

"But the fruit of the Spirit is Love, Joy, Peace, Patience, Kindness, Goodness, Faith, Gentleness, and Self-Control"
(Galatians 5:22-23 ESV)

The ground that produces a luscious crop of fruit, vegetables, and plants has to be tended. There is cultivation that must take place. Whether plowing, sowing, watering, dusting, etc., preparation and maintenance are key elements in ensuring a rich, ripe, and enjoyable harvest, one that is worth multiplying. Getting and keeping the believer willing, ready, and able to yield fruit in due season also requires specific actions to produce the desired results. This feat requires an adequate amount of many things such as prayer, reading the Bible, spending time with God, meditating on His Word, and fellowshipping with other believers. God has created things in such a way that with the right amounts of practices saturated in faith, belief, and sacrifice can bring forth a crop that possesses the power to overcome any foe. However, the believer has the choice to commit to the preparation of service to the glory of God. Without the devotion to the practices — seeking to increase your faith, belief, and committing to sacrifice, you may not be able to be "all in" and fulfill what God expects regarding your purpose.

Let us remember that God doesn't need us to do these things. He wants us to love Him to the point that we desire to do whatever it takes to bring Him glory. He made us His workmanship and created good works specifically for each of us (Ephesians 2:10 NKJV). It is up to us to step up to the plate and do our best to accomplish what He has laid before us.

There will be times when it seems as though there is no way we can do the task set in front of us. We feel like we don't have the strength, resources, motivation, or stamina. We want to give up and just run away — quick, fast, and in a hurry. During these times, the fertilized field begins to yield a return on the efforts performed prior to this very moment. It's when you search your mind and heart for the prayer you prayed, the scripture you read, the time spent with the Lord, and the fellowship with believers that you can hear The Holy Spirit. He is reminding you that you are not alone and never will be. The Holy Spirit is right there telling you that you are more than capable of completing this assignment because it was made for you. You don't have to muster up any extra strength on your own. It is your faith, belief, obedience, and discipline that He needs in order to help you stay ready to bear the fruit required for the situation. As fruit bearers, we will need to fertilize our fields.

Chapter IX

Rest in the Patience

"But the fruit of the Spirit is Love, Joy, Peace, Patience, Kindness, Goodness, Faith, Gentleness, and Self-Control" (Galatians 5:22-23 ESV)

One of the most famous scripture passages, Psalm 23 (KJV), depicts a wonderful illustration of what the enjoyment of patience can look like. "He makes me to lie down in green pastures." You are forced to stop and cease any type of worry or concern. You've left the hustle and bustle behind and have escaped to a place where you are waiting in comfort. Your surroundings are rich and full of potential. They seemed to be prepared for your stay. You were brought here by your trusted Father, who always knows best for His child.

It's not that you have totally disconnected from your world, responsibility, or tasks, but you're preparing for the next step in a calm state of mind. You know this intentional break will produce your best self to accept and walk in whatever outcome your stillness has birthed. You are practicing the ability to release the urge to continuously go non-stop or to insist on receiving input all the time with no break for digestion, comprehension, or reflection. Just going, going, and going.

Patience sees the value in the expression "less is more." Time in inactivity can be productive, and space allowed between one task and the next can create genius. We seem to be in a world where most societies are rushing all the time and sometimes without any direction. The art of patience can birth quality in silence and stillness, which rapid, non-stop movement and talking can't come close to capturing. It's just a fact that we were made to live with pauses. They allow breathing and generating ideas to exist in tandem. The pauses catch what the movement and noise might miss. Patience often creates an environment where a person can take time to evaluate a situation accurately. In this environment, they can observe clues that might expose the absence of an essential element in the current circumstance. This find could drastically change a response or outcome pertaining to important aspects of the person's life or career. In personal and relational instances, patience–taking a breath before responding–can prevent words and actions from being spoken or done that have the potential to be irreparable. Harsh words or wrong accusations can destroy a solid friendship that took years to build in just seconds.

There is wisdom laid up in patience. The Holy Spirit is exact in all His ways. He knows the precise balance of anger, insecurity, bitterness, and fear which might be hovering around a situation. He also knows how much time and reasoning it will take to produce appropriate and loving responses in certain situations. He is depending on you to obey His prompting if you are the one called to exhibit patience. If you are able to influence another regarding their use of patience, He wants you to move in confidence to achieve that result. The difference between waiting five more minutes or not could be the difference in receiving something incredible or something disastrous. Patience represents knowing the time to disengage and accept silence as well as knowing what to do during this period of release. One has to act quickly on the issue at hand if circumstances arise that dictate sudden reengagement. This is critical to properly handling a situation and why keeping an ear open for The Holy Spirit works well. Timing is His specialty.

The world is going faster than it knows and faster than it was created to go. Just because you can do something doesn't mean that it is the thing for YOU to do. In Corinthians 10:23 (NASB), it says, "All things are lawful, but not all things are profitable. All things are lawful, but not all things edify." We can't seem to get our minds to slow down these days. Here we are in today, and our minds are already in the next month trying to solve the "anticipated" problems there. Slow your roll. Such haste and uncontrolled anticipation are far from the pure design God had when creating His children.

Remember, we are to be anxious for nothing (Philippians 4:6 NKJV). Concerns and worries are not to find a resting place in our minds or hearts. We are to carry things that concern, disturb, or challenge us to God in prayer (1 Peter 5:7 KJV). Why do we sometimes, and for some, too often, have difficulty in following this clear instruction? It may be because we resist exercising the patience required to run our race and obtain the expected end God planned for us before the beginning of time.

Do we realize how much we are shortchanging ourselves and our lives, refusing to dump stuff, or better yet, not accumulate it in the first place? Computers have capacities, and once they have reached them, they must delete excess information. We have a preferred capacity and a doable capacity. The preferred capacity can be reached when we operate in God's will. We can experience beauty, ease, and fulfillment of our desires. The doable capacity comes from operating in His permissive will. Yes, it is doable but is it really profitable to His purpose, which is our assignment. Humility can often be our governor to let us know what we will choose to direct our thoughts, feelings, and actions. We were graced with free will, so we can always make a choice, and we do. Making no choice is choosing. All choices affect more than the one making the choice. Exercising patience can provide the time to reflect on the possible outcomes of the choices being contemplated.

We were created to live together, and although we might think we are doing life alone, that is never the case. Someone is always subject to the consequences of our actions. God designed it that way, and He knew exactly what He wanted to accomplish through these connections. Our missteps can have huge and impactful effects on our personal circle of friends and family, our culture, and even our world. Yes, that is right, they can affect our world. We are powerful enough that something we do can alter the entire world. There is something called the "butterfly effect." This theory proposes that a small change can make much bigger changes happen; one small incident can have a big impact on the future. Never underestimate the power God put in you. This is also why it is important to rely on The Holy Spirit to lead your thoughts, feelings, and actions. Abide in Him to get the essentials on how He sees your journey. What destiny does He have for you? What things is He preparing and protecting you for and from? He can tell you your life story and help you walk it out perfectly through a time of abiding with Him.

Our relationships are so important, and God knew it would take everything we had to keep them running smoothly, or at least relatively smooth. One of the most endearing gestures that can be bestowed on another person is to be patient with them. See past your schedule, your intellect, your position, and yourself. Ask for insight from The Holy Spirit as to what that person needs that you could supply. Obey, and you can allow them to see Christ in your actions. You might be the only break they've been able to catch that day. What an impact you could have on that moment. Moments, lead to hours, hours to days, days to years, and years lead to the summation of our lives.

In our society, some people fear not being enough or not knowing enough. People are afraid to show their vulnerabilities to others and oftentimes are in a constant state of fear of rejection or failure. (My story) This is a huge drain on their quality of life. Your conscious effort to slow down and determine where a person may be struggling can render significant effects. This gesture has the potential to help the person see themselves as worthy and increase their self-esteem. It can help them feel more confident in sharing their concerns and lead to better performance. This could have a widespread effect on the person and their family, friends, coworkers, and company. Because you trusted your patience gene, look at what you get to be a part of creating.

With all that is happening in our world today and in times gone by, patience for the believer is paramount. The evidence all around is counter to what we hope. Yet, it is not counter to what God's word has declared. "It declares that there will be wars and rumors of wars, men would be lovers of themselves, people would be against each other" (Matthew 24:6; 2 Timothy 3:2 NKJV). It is a time that our faith is being tested every turn we make. We must determine whether we actually believe what we read or heard at church, Bible study, Sunday school, and small groups. Can we really make it in this world with all the attacks being launched daily, minute by minute on Facebook, Instagram, etc.? Do we truly have what it takes to stand our ground and proclaim what we know about our Lord? Well, patience is revealed best in time. There is a requirement to stop and calm your spirit. Are you willing to train and tame your spirit to honor this requirement in order to receive the best results?

Now, it is difficult to be still in the midst of chaos or danger, or devastation. It is against what our human minds and body want to do. However, in order to manifest the patience necessary for the situation, we have to release the urge to act. We have to let go of the reigns. We have to allow The Holy Spirit to take control of us and disconnect us from whatever is pulling us towards constant action, over-evaluation, and uninformed thought. It doesn't mean that we are not acting, evaluating, or thinking while being patient. However, it does mean the focus of those things has undergone a shift. We are now (or should be) in a place to receive what might not have seemed prudent.

Maybe we are receiving confirmation that the actions we were planning will birth a good outcome. Patience can allow something new or different to enter into our consideration. You feel safe enough to entertain the idea that there could be more to this situation. Exercising patience – taking a step back or pausing for a moment–can also address our physical needs. These are often neglected when we are in full-blown crisis mode.

In 1 Kings 19: 4-10 (NKJV), Elijah suffered from sleep deprivation and hunger. His perception that he was the only one fighting for God almost caused him to ignore all that God had allowed him to accomplish. Just think about what choices and perceptions can come from missing meals and not getting adequate rest. We don't always realize how important it is to take care of our physical needs. Everything God equipped us with serves a purpose in our journey to victory. It all should line up in the prescribed manner to produce optimal execution. A malnourished brain will not produce the best thoughts. Tired feet will not give the support needed to transport from one place to the next. A heart that has been bruised and misused will not create stable emotions in critical situations. It all matters, and patience is key in realizing the balance needed to push through.

In the celebratory times and in the grieving times, patience has a place. It can allow you to reflect on the joy of the moment as well as give you just enough stillness to realize that hope is alive. What it does for you, you are able to transfer to others in your actions. You can bear witness to the power of stepping back and allowing patience to have its perfect work in you (James 1:4 NKJV). It is your victory birthed from patience that makes you so credible to others and the perfect person for The Holy Spirit to use. Patience might accompany you while staying in the hospital with a friend who is unsure whether her loved one will make it through the night. Whether your time is spent in long conversations centered around the person's childhood or unrecognizable speech distorted by uncontrollable crying — patience fortifies you to embrace whatever you encounter. Don't run away from the opportunities to give what you have so divinely been given. Remember, you were specifically crafted for all of your assignments. You have the best coach possible leading you through — The Holy Spirit. Meet Him with patience in your heart.

Fruitful Yield: Patience

Scripture to Read:

Wait on the LORD: be of good courage, and he shall strengthen thine heart: wait, I say, on the LORD

(Psalm 27:14 KJV).

Questions to Answer:

What will be your daily yield of patience today?

Did you see patience displayed today, and if so, how?

Thought to Ponder:

Enjoy the green pastures while God is making the answer available for you.

Chapter X

Tender Touches of Kindness Matter

"But the fruit of the Spirit is Love, Joy, Peace, Patience, Kindness, Goodness, Faith, Gentleness, and Self-Control" (Galatians 5:22-23 ESV)

In today's world, kindness seems to be old-fashioned, outdated, and increasingly inconsequential. It is defined as the quality of being friendly, generous, and considerate. How can such a concept ever be outdated? The truth of the matter is kindness is very much in fashion, needed, and appreciated but often not exhibited. If you're giving someone something they don't expect, you're probably going to catch them off guard, especially if they're having a challenging day. Depending on the level of challenges the day is presenting, their behavior might not be resonating "be kind to me." But this is exactly where kindness belongs. Kindness looks past the behavior and seeks to address the person's need.

Kindness has the ability to change your environment. Kindness is also a multiplier — one act begets another. There is a positive effect on the person generating the act as well as the person receiving it. God knew the multiplying effect of kindness; that is why He put it in your toolkit for achieving His purpose. At least for this moment, something good is happening that perhaps a person didn't anticipate and certainly didn't illicit. Kindness directed towards you helps release any momentary concern and causes you to recognize that someone is paying attention to you, your issue, and your life.

There will be times when a person might not behave in a manner where it is easy to exhibit kindness towards them, but that does not mean kindness should not be shown. For it to be displayed in situations like this, it has to come from someone who knows it is their responsibility and assignment to give it when and where it is needed. As a believer who has relinquished control to The Holy Spirit, you can yield an act of kindness during the most unexpected circumstance because you are not operating in your own power. As we find ourselves in day-to-day situations with people we know, people we don't know, people we wish we didn't know, and people we wish we did know, it is our charge to greet them all with sincere kindness. I think one of the neatest ways to show kindness is when you know a person likes a particular thing and you get it for them. When you present it to them, you instantly create a special moment with them. You have provided them with something that brings them a smile and a feeling of acknowledgment and appreciation. When the days are long, dark, and dreary, having something to pick you up that you did not expect can make a positive difference in one's life.

What happened during that moment? Through this act of kindness, the love of Christ is on display. The beneficiary of the act is seeing, feeling, and, possibly, touching what it feels like to have Christ in their life. This might be tough for them to receive, especially if they have not demonstrated action worthy of such kindness.

The account of Hosea and Gomer is a great illustration of how kindness can be shown in situations that from the outside may be hard to justify. God told Hosea to marry Gomer although she was a known harlot. Hosea obeyed God and married (Hosea 1:2-3 NKJV). Gomer left Hosea. Hosea was directed to bring Gomer back home. He had to purchase her from her current benefactor. The scriptures indicate that Gomer had been enslaved and had relations with others besides Hosea, but he showed incredible kindness, as well as his love and respect for God, by bringing her back and accepting her into the family once again. There are probably very few men who would be willing to follow God's instruction to bring her back home. Her behavior surely didn't warrant such kindness, but that did not matter. God commanded this act, and that settled the issue for Hosea.

A person's worthiness is not part of the equation when speaking about bearing the fruit through The Holy Spirit. Man has no place to judge, just yield to the direction of The Holy Spirit. In this, you are also giving witness to an example of a person freely giving The Holy Spirit access in their lives. Offering access to The Holy Spirit is not done because believers are so worthy. We are not worthy, but we do have the righteousness of God through Christ (2 Corinthians 5:21). This makes the difference. Due to such power, a precious attitude of kindness can change the entire dynamics of a situation. In life, the truth can be stranger than fiction, especially God's truth.

As I was writing this book, I took a trip to Atlanta to see relatives. On the way, there were some bumps in the road during my trip. I got two flat tires, and my battery died. Mind you, I was driving a rental car. I started this section of the book right before my first flat tire. The Lord knew that

I would need to be clothed with a mindset of kindness to manage this frustrating and disappointing situation. While dealing with the dilemma, it would have been so easy to have a tone in my voice that was not kind, thoughtful, or professional, but I didn't have to worry about any missteps. The Holy Spirit, who is always striving on our side, took over.

Just writing this section was part of the preparation offered to get me ready to demonstrate kindness towards people who were just there to help me. They were not responsible for my situation, and addressing them with a tone of arrogance or rudeness would have been contrary to what God wants displayed by His children. This type of preparation comes from those practices of fertilizing our fields. Remember, we are reaping what we sow. It's not always the actual action that is done that is so critical — it is the mindset, the thought, the willingness to consider doing things that are caring, compassionate, and thoughtful for others. God is all-knowing and is aware of the magnificent power of a kind word. He has knowledge of every detail in a person's life. What might seem trivial or not necessary to us, He knows what significance it bears. The protection it can bring. The decision it can thwart. The life it can save.

Obeying The Holy Spirit's urgings and guidance will become more natural and spontaneous the more you abide in the Word and spend time with God. This can assist in our execution of kindness when it is most needed, and that could be a time when we least want to give it! However, keep in mind, you are on assignment to do your part in creating fruitful living widespread, embracing others and their concerns, and being on one accord. Kindness is a surefire strategy to reach this end.

Fruitful Yield: Kindness

Scripture to Read:

Let not mercy and truth forsake thee: bind them about thy neck; write them upon the table of thine heart

(Proverbs 3:3 KJV)

Questions to Answer:

What will be your yield of kindness today?

Did you see kindness displayed today, and if so, how?

Thought to Ponder:

Let the fragrance of kindness linger long after your presence has vacated the premises.

Chapter XI

Great is Thy Goodness

"But the fruit of the Spirit is Love, Joy, Peace, Patience, Kindness, Goodness, Faith, Gentleness, and Self-Control"
(Galatians 5:22-23 ESV)

God is good, and every believer is made in His image. Therefore, you are good. God has given believers the gift of possessing goodness. Your display of this trait brings the very nature of God to the situation.

A definition of goodness is an uprightness of heart and life, the quality of being morally good or virtuous. This sets the framework for your thoughts, feelings, and actions. This includes how you talk to people, treat people, and protect and defend people. Civility is important to God. He saved us to exist in a communal world. Goodness aims to make certain that our existence with others is amenable, profitable, sustainable, and relevant to His purpose — bringing Heaven to earth.

In Psalm 107 (NKJV), God shows His goodness and mercy to those He loves. The very redemption God provided for us from the enemy portrays a resounding example and image of virtue. The passage recounts numerous situations where man has fallen into peril, but God delivered him. Whether it was from wandering in the wilderness, languishing in prison, enduring sickness, or tossing on a stormy sea, God delivered. He didn't have to do it, but He did.

God's goodness is loving and just. There is balance in His work, and He has specific expectations. In that same scripture, Psalm 107: 33-34 (NKJV), it illustrates that God can turn rivers into a wilderness, and the springs into dry ground; a fruitful land into barrenness, for the wickedness of those who dwell in it. There will be repercussions for not following the mandates of God, and they can be quite severe. Aren't you glad that The Holy Spirit also works in us to help the believer follow principles that God expects us to demonstrate? As with everything, we choose what direction or actions we will take.

Another example of Jesus' goodness is that of the woman caught in the act of adultery. In John 8:1-11(NKJV), we see Jesus coming to the aid of a woman who has been dragged from a compromising position to the town to be judged. In those days, the punishment for adultery was stoning. Jesus was asked how this woman should be judged. It is written that after a period of silence, Jesus bent down and started to write on the ground with his finger. We do not know what he wrote. We just know the reaction that followed. After being hammered with questions, Jesus asked that the person with no sin throw the first stone. Upon this statement being made, the people began to disperse. There was no one without sin. When Jesus looked around, it was only He and the woman. He told her that He didn't condemn her and that she should go and sin no more. What wisdom, compassion, and goodness Jesus displayed. We all have sinned and fallen short of the glory of God (Romans 3:23 NKJV). The problem is that so many of us seem to forget this fact. In His deliberation, we see that Jesus pondered before taking action. This is a good practice to adopt. Allow The Holy Spirit to prompt you and other believers to bring to remembrance past mistakes and God's past, current, and future grace. Let's do what Jesus did — extend goodness and grace.

Allowing others to feel God's goodness through caring for them is an loving activity. Goodness in word and deed is one of the most authentic ways to show true concern. Being conscious of what is beneficial for the whole and not just the individual is important in executing goodness. We must consider what will bring about justice, wholesomeness, safe dwelling, and collective prosperity among the land. Believers are called to play a significant role in supporting others in their survival and helping them reach a point of thriving. It is at this point that humility should take the reins.

Thinking about ourselves less and yielding to the directions of The Holy Spirit about the needs of others is how we can produce the goodness needed to transform our spaces and communities. Many feel that humble people are weak, mild, and insufficient. However, we know that the most important act of humility ever performed was from the most powerful person in the world. When Jesus gave His life for us, He was truly thinking of Himself less. He was thinking of the rich rewards that would be gained by this act of humility and obedience to the Father. Having the mind of Christ increases the probability of us displaying such goodness on our path.

Oftentimes people are confused between goodness and kindness. The primary difference between the two is that goodness involves righteousness in action or doing what is right. Kindness involves being generous, considerate, and helping others. Although for some, kindness seems to be more valued because it is often associated with outward expressions. Goodness permeates the believer's thoughts, feelings, and actions. The actions that goodness births can be far-reaching and influence many.

Regarding God's desire to have His children be fruitful and multiply, people motivated by goodness can be influential catalysts for the greater good. They often see the bigger picture and are willing to go the extra mile to reach common ground. Such a trait is very desirable in those tasked with making laws, policies, and practices for the good of the whole.

In society, there are many situations where people are encouraged to concentrate on their differences instead of what could be best for the group. This could delay the progress of God's plan for His creation to live in unity and prosper if it were not for The Holy Spirit. Remember, you are not bearing these traits in your own strength. We have the power of God through The Holy Spirit to put us in just the right place at the right time to do what is best in God's eyes. Sure, this can be scary and stressful. However, we are protected by the best Helper created. Goodness will prevail, and God's goodness towards us will prevail.

When dealing with circumstances involving many people, groupthink can rob us of acts of goodness. People get comfortable not doing the right thing because no one else is stepping up. As a believer, you get the privilege to let The Holy Spirit help you to be the one who demonstrates goodness. The one who makes the situation better and doesn't just let things get swept under the carpet. The world is in dire need of carriers of goodness, and God has equipped His children to fill this need.

Goodness displayed makes the heart well. In a world that is running fast and often guided by self-interest and greed, a person's display of goodness can benefit many. Whether this goodness takes the form of supporting a charity, getting signatures for a petition to shut down a crack house, an employer adding more paid holidays, or other acts of goodness, those who reap the benefits feel the effects. They no longer feel like just a number. They can see and sense that there are those concerned about their existence, survival, success, and legacy. With these intentional demonstrations, they are experiencing the goodness of God. Aren't you glad to be part of such work for the Kingdom? After all, it is stated that God made him who had no sin to be sin for us, so that in him we might become the righteousness of God (2 Corinthians 5:21 NIV). We are here to show what is right through our acts of goodness.

Fruitful Yield: Goodness

Scripture to Read:

Neither do men light a candle, and put it under a bushel, but on a candlestick; and it giveth light unto all that are in the house. Let your light so shine before men, that they may see your good works, and glorify your Father which is in heaven (Matthew 5:15-16 KJV).

Questions to Answer:

What will be your yield of goodness today?

Did you see goodness displayed today, and if so, how?

Thought to Ponder:

The caring of others' welfare reflects God's portrait of humanity.

Chapter XII

Deep Rooting
(Sustaining your Power)

---●————————●————————●---

"But the fruit of the Spirit is Love, Joy, Peace, Patience, Kindness, Goodness, Faith, Gentleness, and Self- Control" (Galatians 5:22-23 ESV)

Have you ever seen the tall trees blowing in the wind and wondered how they could withstand the wind and not come tumbling down? Well, it's because their roots are so deep! God knows all the gale winds, hurricanes, trials, misfortunes, and what seems to be just bad luck that will encroach into your life. He is aware that there will be times when nothing seems like it is working, and you may feel as though you are the one who is responsible for getting everything to work, and perfectly at that. Nothing escapes Him. He has prepared you for every moment you will face and has given you the resources needed to face and overcome the situations. We have to realize that the overcoming might not look like what we had in mind, but God has the final say. He knows what it takes to achieve His goal. You will need to saturate yourself in humility, compassion, and fidelity to develop the ability to produce–at the most tender urging of The Holy Spirit–whatever fruit is needed. By this, you bring God into the situation and accomplish His purpose of fruitful living on earth. You are the container of great power; sustaining your capacity for this work is a top priority.

God knows what it takes to bring you to the point where you can receive the ability and inclination to ward off the feelings of overwhelming despair and hopelessness when in challenging or seemingly impossible circumstances. You can't do it in your own strength. This is why He has equipped you with your constant companion, The Holy Spirit. The Holy Spirit is well able to direct your path to safety in all circumstances. You have access to Him constantly, and because of your deep-rooted practices, you will begin to recognize Him more and use His power more frequently and naturally. From your Bible reading, you know the mighty acts performed by and through The Holy Spirit. You saw people who needed just a push to accomplish their goal, and through prayer and earnest belief, they were able to win. Whatever is needed, The Holy Spirit supplies. You just have to be open and call on Him.

Although it seems like there is lots of activity going on during this rooting process, one of the most crucial things that must be done is welcoming silence. Yes, the noise and responsibilities of the current environment might have you thinking, Silence? Give me a break. How can I get quiet when you have me doing all these other things? While it's not necessarily easy, it is achievable. It is essential in making all the other activities produce the expected results. In silence, you can best hear and heed the urging of The Holy Spirit. All the other noise represents outside activities or influences. Silence makes that which is internal more noticeable and accessible. You can commune with The Holy Spirit and capture what He is saying or how He is directing you. Keep in mind, God knows all. Whatever He gives you is for the perfect solution. There is surety in The Holy Spirit. Doubt, worry, fear, they have no true victory in the presence of The Holy Spirit because, like the Father, He is omnipotent, omnipresent, and omniscient. You are in good hands with The Holy Spirit. Release anything holding you back or causing you to believe that you are not on the right path when you are in communion with The Holy Spirit.

Reflect on God's love and believe that you are able to produce a harvest of obedience and receptivity when you follow the prompting of The Holy Spirit. The returns of such a yield are all around you. Just look. God gave us all memories, but sometimes, we don't use our memories as effectively concerning our faith walk. The reward of obedience and the reaction of disobedience are both evident in your life if you just take a moment to reflect. Over the past few days, you can probably recall a decision made in obedience and the outcome rendered. How happy were you that you made the right choice? One that God was pleased with and a decision that supported His purpose.

On the other hand, there might also be a decision made that you are still regretting because it came from resisting The Holy Spirit's calling. It was based totally on your desire and your need for a particular result. Take a moment and evaluate how each outcome affected you – your thoughts, feelings, actions. Can you truly say it was worth choosing the decision which was birthed out of disobedience? An important point to note here is that it is always your choice. The Heavenly Father has given you free will, and even if He knows your choice will lead to a disastrous end, He is not going to interfere. He has given you the permission to make a choice and will let you run with it, but never alone.

The urgings of The Holy Spirit are God's directions which lead to His perfect will. Covering yourself with prayer, Bible reading, time with God in silence, and meditation on the Word helps to gain strength, conviction, and tenacity to choose the will of God. This secures the best outcome for all. You will be subject to distractions and disruptions as you plunge yourself into devoted time connecting with the Father. Be ready to combat those interferences because the things that keep you wanting more of Him are going to give you the sure footing when the rubber meets the road, and you are required to move into action.

The best time to go deep is when you are free from enormous pressure. You have the flexibility to schedule the activities and support in your daily agenda. At this time, there is no emergency altering your ability to make good choices. You are free to spend more time in silence, reading your Bible, meditating on the Word, praying in the spirit, and giving extra attention to those around you. It is actually inviting, and enjoyable and best of all, you and others will notice the difference in you — your talk, walk, and heart will begin to resemble God's character.

In the book of James, it says to know better and not do it is a sin. If you ignore the necessity of strengthening your inner man and spending more time with God so He can build you up, you run the risk of not being able to reach the level it's going to take for you to withstand the attacks that are to come. Also, not being ready with a level of confidence to respond in situations where you are the influencer for someone else to see God's preferred response or outcome. God's love, the fullness of our Father's essence, should really be enough to drive us to please Him 24/7. The greatness of this love is incomprehensible to man, yet there is overwhelming evidence of its magnitude. Don't let your pace be so fast; you can't see, feel, experience the intensity of God's love for you. It is this love that will propel you to accept the direction of The Holy Spirit, the one He personally sent to and for you.

Prioritization is key. Who and what will receive your best? Your consistent, in-depth study of the scriptures, your time spent with fellow believers, your worship and fellowship in your house of worship, or your sacred space at your home are all essential parts to molding and sustaining the level of faith, belief, and commitment to stay ready to do the will of God. Don't ever lose sight of how much God loves you and sees you as an integral part of His plan. Your obedience is critical to His perfect will. Ask The Holy Spirit to shepherd your decision-making when determining the order of your actions.

Developing the mind of Christ is our ultimate goal. When this is in progress, we readily delight in pleasing God without any hesitation. We run with anticipation to do, be, and say, "thus saith the Lord." This comes from transforming into a being who freely gives their life for their Father's purpose because they understand the depth of His love. This reaction is directly related to the kind of love we see that Christ received from God. He had no question about how much His Father valued him or the worth He bestowed on him. He knew no greater love could or would ever exist. When you are assured of love at such a level, you are ready to move mountains to sustain it. The assurance of that kind of bond derives from a variety of sources. The scriptures serve to expose the love of God to His people. Through chapter and verse, we can see how God protected, guided, strengthened, chastened, and loved His creation. He has never stopped doing this, and He never will.

There are times when what we are receiving doesn't feel so loving. Take, for instance, the escapades I shared about my trip to Atlanta with the two flat tires and dead battery. I was in amazement at how all that was working for my good! But it was. This adventure could have easily ended differently.

During daily commuting from home to work, there are numerous inherent dangers possible in that journey. When traveling out of state, on major highways, and unfamiliar surroundings, you can multiply that by ten. My trip added car trouble and six o'clock traffic all around me on the highway. While experiencing the unfolding of events that started at the rental pick-up in Jacksonville, Florida, I can say I continued to see the hand of God. From the help of a stranger letting me know I had a flat tire, to the manager at the local tire shop who made time to replace the tire, to a fellow driver who let me know I was driving on I-75 North with a flat tire (mind you this was less than ninety minutes from when the other tire was replaced).

The wonders continued with having a concerned AAA dispatcher prioritize my issue because the three other requests had been canceled, to having a hotel close by where I could charge my phone because the gas station clerk refused to allow me to use the outlet, to my elderly aunt and uncle making their way over 30 miles to pick me up while I left the rental car there alone to be towed to their home. Yes, every step of the way, God was there. Having protected the Truth of God and His word in my heart with a deeper acknowledgment of The Holy Spirit, I was able to know that I would not perish during this crisis. I would be alright, physically, emotionally, and spiritually. We can always be confident that it is in our best interest if it is coming from God. He only desires us to be the person He designed us to become.

God has stationed people on our path to sharpen us. The Bible tells us that as iron sharpens iron, so one person sharpens another (Proverb 27:17 NIV). When we greet those around us with the right attitude, we can benefit from our Christian growth. It is not by accident that we find ourselves surrounded by certain people. It is all by His design to help us along in the process of becoming more like Christ. When we are afforded the privilege to see Christ in the actions and attitudes of others, it builds our belief that we can be more like Christ. Likewise, when we have the nature of God on full display, others are encouraged that they can attain the same.

God knows that what He is asking in certain circumstances may seem impossible or, at least, very difficult. As humans, we often doubt our ability to do what is expected. God knew there would be doubt, worry, and fear. He already accounted for those times when we are gripped with enormous fear and dread and can't seem to break free. We can't seem to hear anything but the pounding of our hearts and the shallow breathing. In times like these, the effects of the deep rooting activate. Through the power of The Holy Spirit, we remember what we have learned. Our breathing slows down. Our heart ceases to sound as loud. Our memory recalls a past situation that implored similar responses but was overcome by calling on our trust and faith in God — believing Him for victory.

As you recall the past victory, you recognize this wasn't someone else's story. This was your story. It was real, relevant, and recent. Following the direction of The Holy Spirit in your current situation should seem natural, or at least there should be a trust factor present to persuade your efforts. Know that you are chosen for this assignment. God has already made you His masterpiece specifically for a multitude of works He has created for you. Following Him, you can't go wrong. This assurance is what you must hold on to. It doesn't matter what it takes to get there; just get there and stay. Eventually, it will take less stress and thought to achieve this state because of the evolution of your transformation. Little by little, you are becoming more like Christ. Just think, you doubted it could happen but see what God, The Holy Spirit, and you have been up to on your journey! Amazing stuff. Keep up the rooting. It pays off.

Chapter XIII

Fortitude of Faithfulness

●────────●────────●

"But the fruit of the Spirit is Love, Joy, Peace, Patience, Kindness, Goodness, Faith, Gentleness, and Self- Control" (Galatians 5:22-23 ESV)

Although not listed first, faith is undoubtedly one trait that increases the likelihood of exercising all the others. Faith is defined as complete trust or confidence in someone or something. For the believer, the someone or something is God, our Father. Other words used to describe faith are firm persuasion, assurance, firm conviction, or faithfulness. These all illustrate the strength associated with faith—the capacity to withstand great force or pressure in the midst of uncertainty. When you have to stand and make a difficult decision without possessing experience or having concrete evidence, you have to pull from a source that you believe will guide you in the right direction and keep you regardless of the choice made. This is why believers choose to have faith in God. The only omniscient, omnipotent, and omnipresent being ever to exist.

When I started this chapter, the Lord had me on Hwy 155 in McDonough, GA, in a rental car, stopped at a BP gas station with one of the two flat tires that occurred that day and a dead battery. I was on my way to Atlanta to visit my aunt and uncle, who I had not seen since prior to COVID 19, the pandemic that took the world by surprise. I knew God blesses families and our efforts to show concern and love towards those He has given to us. I wasn't quite sure what this current faith test was targeting.

Unemployed, I was taking time, now available, to check up on my older relatives, make some new memories, discuss career opportunities, just fellowship, eat, and laugh. I didn't expect to encounter two flat tires along the way, cross I-75 North from the far-left lane to the far-right lane on a Friday at 5:30 pm due to the second flat tire, request support from AAA three separate times, and finally have my elderly relatives, who live 30 miles away, come pick me up at a BP station at 11:00 p.m. It all seemed somewhat strange, certainly not what I expected at 8:30 am that morning when I left my house to pick up the rental car.

We know we are targeted for spiritual warfare, and that comes from being one of God's children, especially those making more effort and attempting to follow His still, small voice. One that is coming to Him with requests for wisdom and approval and boldly and publicly sharing their love for the Father. Although we know we have favor with God, we might ask why this "trust experience" has appeared at this moment. We are walking closer than ever with The Holy Spirit and sensing His presence evermore. We are asking for wisdom and hearing from God on whether or not the choices we are contemplating are in His will. However, it seems like, on this particular day, there is a lot facing me. But why should this day not have a lot in it?

My experience was that I was drawing closer to God, and therefore, He was drawing closer to me. He was letting me study more, read more, understand more, and feel more. I woke up every morning ready to jump out of bed and onto my knees and give Him thanks. God gave me songs that He created in that second and confidence to keep the routine that was created to frame the days with gladness, hope, peace, and productivity. Yes, He tells me that abiding in Him gives me the strength that cannot be described in mere words. It's His words coming alive and witnessing the truths that fill these pages. His love for me makes it easy for me to want to spend more time with Him. I want to understand God's precepts so that I can integrate them into my walk. A walk aimed at inviting others to experience the magnificence of being in His presence where there is assurance that all is always well. It is from the abiding that I am able to get to the stage of delighting in Him.

Embracing every thought, He brings to mind, captivated by the mighty feats He displayed in the pages of the greatest story ever told. How easy it is to desire more of someone like this.

Consistently hearing His Word has allowed my faith and belief in God to grow immensely. I have confidence in the belief that He is who He said He is and that He will do what He said He would do. What an honor that He sees me as one who will attempt to do what He said would be done! That's why there should be little room for certain questions. Why? How can this happen? The questions that will solidify my faith are: What am I to learn from this? How should I respond? Is there significance in the timing of this occurrence? What truth will be revealed through my thoughts, feelings, and actions? When will I know that I've represented God well? When will I know I've stepped out on my own? Did I read the clues from my last revelation correctly?

After walking with God for some time, you might think there should be no room for questions of doubt. That all the questions would focus on spiritual growth. But the truth is that this faith of mine still seems to falter many times. I am positive that God believes in me. But I don't believe in me. God has created me for this moment, this challenge, this reward. But am I following through with it or embracing it? The question replaying in my mind is, "How is this really going to work out for any good?" But then God demonstrates exactly why I am able to navigate back to Him with my seemingly inconsequential level of faith. It's because He knows He provided all I need to grow my faith in Him. God has provided His word and my Helper, The Holy Spirit, to me. He knows that there is nothing else in life that can win over Him. God has control of everything and has decided to love me in an incomprehensible manner. One I can never understand, nor ever deny.

So, the truth is faith grows by our working our faith, allowing it to prove itself. How do we know we have faith if we have never had to believe in something we don't see? If our senses confirm everything for us, there is no need for further clarification. The opportunity to use the gift of hope to embrace something that is not currently present does not exist. The advantages received when our faith is being built are immense. Faith in action can move mountains, walk through cancer, believe for wisdom, say goodbye to loved ones with sorrow but not regret, take over projects that you have no experience in doing but the opportunity found you, and speak truth to power in love with total conviction.

Let's briefly look at Joseph's faith. In the article, Joseph–A Life of Faithfulness by Jeff Simmons, he reminds us that one-third of the Old Testament is dedicated to Joseph and his faith walk. He highlights five lessons we can learn from studying Joseph's life. They are "Life is not Easy," "Integrity Matters," "Trust in God's Sovereignty," "Forgive and Love Always," and "God is Greater." In the first lesson, "Life is not Easy," we see that he didn't have it easy, although Joseph was born into a family of wealth and stature. His father, Jacob, loved Joseph more than he did his other sons, and this played out through his unparalleled actions towards his son. This caused great contention between Joseph and his siblings and eventually led to them selling him into slavery. Although astonished, terrified, and alone, Joseph doesn't give up as he is taken to unfamiliar territory. He keeps pressing on.

The second lesson, "Integrity Matters," is revealed when Joseph is continuously approached by Potiphar's wife. On one occasion, she takes advantage of being alone with him and tries to seduce him. Joseph, knowing what is right in the eyes of God and that his master has entrusted him with all his household, removes himself from the situation. But his coat is left behind. Out of anger and embarrassment, Potiphar's wife accuses Joseph of attacking her, and his act of integrity lands him in prison. Yet, Joseph continues to believe and executes his responsibilities to the glory of God. Doing the right things hadn't seemed to be getting Joseph any gains on the surface.

The third lesson, "Trust in God's Sovereignty," demonstrates that we are often unaware of how God's ultimate plans are going to work out in our lives. We must continue to build our faith and let it be our guide. Joseph went from prison to eventually becoming the second in command over all of Egypt. His faith proved worthy of God's honor and propelled him into places he had no idea he would occupy. God used every situation in Joseph's life to prepare him for the next appointment. With God, nothing we go through is wasted. It is all part of His plan for His children as they seek to live out His purpose.

In the fourth lesson, "Forgive and Love Always," Joseph is able to demonstrate the power of the fruit of love and faith. After about twenty years from being sold by his brothers, Joseph has an encounter with them when they come to Egypt to buy food during a famine. They were under the impression that Joseph had died and had no idea that the person they were bowing down to was their little brother. Once they were aware of his identity, they thought surely, he would have them killed, but Joseph's decision after wrestling with God was to do just the opposite. He forgave them, and eventually, they came to live with him in Egypt. Joseph's forgiveness demonstrated the trait of love. It's the one thing that changes everything.

The final lesson, "God is Greater," shows us that Joseph consistently had God as his main focus throughout his entire life. In every situation reflected, he made decisions based on his respect and understanding of God and God's power and purpose in his life. Regarding Joseph's reunion with his brothers, he tells them in Genesis 50:20 (NIV), "You intended to harm me, but God intended it for good to accomplish what is now being done, the saving of many lives." When we honor God with our thoughts, feelings, and actions, He honors us with His riches. He is always up to good for His children. Keep walking in the faith, and you will not be dissatisfied.

Let us be reminded that it was in his home that Joseph first observed the importance of having faith in God. Knowing His ways and expectations, Jacob's conduct and manner contributed to Joseph's solid foundation of faith in our God. This love from his earthly father led to animosity from his brothers, which gave Joseph a glimpse of what it meant to be loved by the almighty God. No matter what Jacob's shortcoming may have been, he gets a grade of A for showing his son how to believe in God at all times.

Joseph's faithfulness is a good illustration of a life that honors God and invokes a response of "Well done, My good and faithful servant"(Matthew 25:21 NIV). Let us all conduct our lives such that we are among those who receive such accolades from Our Father because of our faith.

Fruitful Yield: Faithfulness

Scripture to Read:

If we are faithless, He remains faithful; He cannot deny Himself (2 Timothy 2:13 NKJV).

Questions to Answer:

What will be your yield of faithfulness today?

Did you see faithfulness displayed today, and if so, how?

Thought to Ponder:

God has a rescue plan for every situation you will face. He's got you.

Chapter XIV

The Embrace of Gentleness Endures

●────────●────────●

"But the fruit of the Spirit is Love, Joy, Peace, Patience, Kindness, Goodness, Faith, Gentleness, and Self-Control" (Galatians 5:22-23 ESV)

Oh, how we long for just the smallest reflection of gentleness in our weakest hour. However, there are times where we don't seem to find it. Such a sad commentary when we think of what gentleness means. One definition says it is the quality of being kind, tender, or mild-mannered. Isn't that something all of us could surely use from time to time?

Yes, the world is hard sometimes. Getting hit from all sides. Waking up to have the best day of your life and then that not being the outcome that unfolded. Facing a very hard challenge and scared of what you will have to be exposed to if you go through. Skipping out on life because you don't want to face what might be waiting for you or, even worse, chasing after you. Wouldn't it be great that when your heart is racing due to over exhaustion and fear that you have a safe place to run to and find a welcoming spirit? Or perhaps a soft word — a tone that is accepting and not accusatory. What about a look that says, "Glad you got this far!" All of these gestures and actions may represent the support you need to find refuge in the moment.

We often beat ourselves up for not knowing something or not being able to perform the way others appear to master a task. The hurt and harm that can be done to our self-image and self- esteem by continuously "uploading" a negative report in our mind produces a damaging imprint. I know this from personal experience. Some of the effects of such a reaction have stayed with me much longer than what would be considered healthy. It is bad enough that we do this to ourselves, but when we have to encounter the same treatment and evaluation from others, it is a heavy burden. This has the effect of weighing us down instead of elevating us to the places God wants.

As believers, we are in partnership with God to assist in creating an atmosphere for fruitful living. In that vein, our humility allows us to be freely led by The Holy Spirit to exhibit whatever characteristic deemed necessary by The Holy Spirit. To be chosen for such a monumental task and important place in Kingdom building can take our breaths away and give us the confidence to walk tall and wait in expectation for the next nudging, waiting not in vain but in preparation.

The fruit of the Spirit resides in all believers from the moment they decide to follow Christ. It is The Holy Spirit that perfects the execution of the fruit. It is important that we create the environment and setting for that execution to be spot on. Feeding the mind and heart with the Word to increase our knowledge of God and His precepts is a great practice when consistently preparing to receive The Holy Spirit's direction. Abstaining from indulging in foods that weaken and advance disease to our bodies also provides important benefits. Actively seeking situations that can be positively influenced by an expression of fruit from the believer is also a worthy activity. As you see, the waiting is not passive but preparatory — not in vain but with victory in sight. Not boring, but a bold declaration that you can complete your chosen assignment.

According to Proverbs 18:21(NKJV), "life and death are in the power of the tongue." People believe what they see others doing. Valuing and accepting a person solely based on the mistakes they made dismisses God's grace in that person's life as well as in ours. When bearing fruit in the right season, for the right situation, at the right time, it will influence our speech, the way we act, and the way we touch others. We should seek to be sure that the purest forms of fruit are presented when directed by The Holy Spirit. The manifestation of the fruit has the power of God to reverse a situation, restore a heart and mind, build and increase belief such that the person can see themselves achieving what has been placed before them. They have the confidence to push through and be a conduit to a greater outcome. It is funny how just displaying tenderness in a moment of frustration or leniency during a rugged patch in someone's life can actually increase their confidence and inspiration to do better. When a person produces a less than stellar outcome, the harsh word and demeaning comments can crush the spirit and permanently damage their ability to reach the potential stored within. It might not be easy, but we don't have to concern ourselves about whether we can supply it; The Holy Spirit has already guaranteed that it's possible.

Our commitment to stay ready for execution is what needs to be solid. Making sure we abide in God's Word and reap the power flowing from His abiding in us is the primary strategy in being ready to answer the call to bear. Your abiding can also make you more sensitive to conditions that serve to alert you that a need exists. Bringing comfort and relief to that situation can be just the right tool to show how God works in your life. It might be enough to spark an interest in a non-believer, such that they will want to know more about what makes you act the way you do. Caring for their needs. Giving a soft landing when a bed of brick would have been the expected response. Forgiving an offense when it seems you are well within your rights to harbor resentment. Remember, as believers, you follow a different set of rules. Gentleness is part of your nature.

It's amazing to think that God, an incomprehensible being, allows us to bear fruit in tangible ways that demonstrate His glory. Sometimes this fruit appears in the most unexpected ways and at the most unimaginable moments. To be part of this equation is extraordinary. God had your role in these countless opportunities before you were a thought in the minds of your parents. He has always had big plans for you — plans to bring His huge desires to fruition. These actions demonstrate and give hope to those who might have lost heart or simply do not know how to exhibit such characteristics or responses.

Your display might be the only evidence for them that people can care for others and still have plenty to provide for their own abundant lives. I want you to be excited that you have been chosen for this auspicious work. God would not assign it to anyone who was not capable of completing it with The Holy Spirit's leading. You might think that your actions don't matter. That no one could ever be influenced by what you say or do, but you are wrong. In our universe, we are all connected, and what one does affects so many others. You may not personally know everyone impacted by your actions, but that doesn't discount the fact that you influenced their lives. Build your belief that God is truth and what He says is so. You have to believe Him because of who He is and not doubt His word or count on your mind to rationalize the answer or guess the probable outcome. His ways are not ours, and therefore we should rely on Him even when we do not know what that result is going to be.

You can see why robing ourselves with humility is so vital because we have to stand in the truth that this assignment is not about me. It is about being a willing vessel for God and His plan. Our understanding doesn't produce truth. Nor does it guarantee the appropriate response. It might not come up with the correct choice to change a life or destiny. But God's word and commands can do all that. Waiting in a prepared and humble state is your posture for pleasing God and displaying traits in their right season. With your grace through gentleness, a person can find greatness. They can be set free to find their significance by overcoming a less than stellar performance and evaluating and recalibrating to a level where that potential can be developed.

Their self-confidence can increase because they didn't have to go through trying to pick themselves up from the ground after the letdown from a person they held in high regard. No, because of your obedience, they didn't have to suffer that disgrace alone. Their belief in themselves and their capabilities start to surface, and they grow right in front of your eyes. Their gratitude is the fuel keeping them forging through. That's what you can be a part of through your gift of gentleness. Making such a reaction a normal occurrence instead of a rare response can change the entire atmosphere — giving people the freedom to try again. Surely this could lead them to know more about what or who influences your actions. This response is what is desired, their seeking the Father.

Fruitful Yield: Gentleness

Scripture to Read:

Pleasant words are as a honeycomb, sweet to the soul, and health to the bones (Proverbs 16:24 KJV).

Questions to Answer:

What will be your yield of gentleness today?

Did you see gentleness displayed today, and if so, how?

Thought to Ponder:

Gentleness increases the possibility of greatness in some of the most unlikely places and sources.

Chapter XV

Surrendering to Self-Control Allows for Withstanding

●━━━━━●━━━━━●

"But the fruit of the Spirit is Love, Joy, Peace, Patience, Kindness, Goodness, Faith, Gentleness, and Self-Control"
(Galatians 5:22-23 ESV)

The last trait is one that is most needed and the one that most of us consistently struggle to exhibit. I have heard love and self-control, or temperance, are called the bookends of the fruit of the Spirit. These two hold the others together. Self-control is defined as the ability to control oneself, particularly one's emotions and desires or the expression of them in one's behavior, especially in difficult situations. It is discipline in the face of pressure from an immediate urge, desire, or compulsion. Literally, this characteristic is needed in every part of your life. Our motives, actions, and decisions determine our lives. It is critical that we are able to make wise, sound judgments regarding how we will proceed in everything.

How do we increase the probability that our actions, decisions, and judgments will be sound? Well, maybe relinquishing some of that control of "self" is a great start. But who freely wants to give up their control? In this world that is driven by self-promotion, self-sufficiency, and Self-reliance, people would think you were foolish to relinquish your power. The world thinks that's what defines you, right? So many have bought into this line of thinking and have led lives with the only aim of satisfying self and glorifying self. For the world, this might be acceptable, however the believer knows this is not of God.

Remember, you are not of this world (John 17:14-16 NKJV). Your value doesn't come from the same claims made by those who don't know, trust, and follow Jesus. Your value comes from the love bestowed on you by God. When you are confronted with a situation that requires strength, intellect, or connection that you don't seem to possess, what is your go-to? What do you do? What thoughts go through your mind? You rely on the source you know has always been there. God, offering you all you need through The Holy Spirit. You exercise your faith to believe you can receive what is required for what you are facing. You, as a believer, may be aware that these things are not coming from you. So, you can graciously accept them from the Source.

In some instances, you might bite your tongue, hold your peace, and dismiss your own assessment of the situation. For those times when you are facing a familiar scenario, which in the past produced a good outcome with the help of The Holy Spirit, you are comfortable with your actions. They have been proven. However, what about those things that push you harder, farther? They make you doubt your ability and sometimes your worth. How do you get these things done? Well, not in your strength. Not in your current knowledge. In a receptive posture, you can await a download from your Helper, The Holy Spirit. The one that makes the scripture "I can do all things through Christ who strengthens me" come to life.

So, how easy is it to stand and wait, restraining yourself from acting on your impulse? Trusting and obeying, even though you are just not sure you will have enough information in time to make the right decision. Let your faith overrule your fear. Surrender. Surrender all within you and allow The Holy Spirit to take control and give you what is needed.

Some people internalize waiting on The Holy Spirit to empower them as meaning they are less than. Not good enough or aren't making the grade. They may think their worth is diminished. In certain cases, their pride might cause them to accept a lesser view of themselves. Nothing could be further from the truth. When you yield to The Holy Spirit, and you welcome His presence with the power, stamina, knowledge, and wisdom all wrapped up in God's love, you are the most valuable to God. You are super worthy of being called a child of God. He created you to provide for any and all of your needs. Waiting for the perfect solution from the Helper exemplifies the righteousness given by Jesus Christ. At that moment, you are shining in front of the Father. He can use you.

The toughest things in life actually require the believer to not show stern might but quiet resolve. You can release control, pride, and visible force, so that the power that moves mountains and raises the dead can show up and tackle the situation through you. Your faith can trigger you to drop the reigns of control and give them to the Lord. Such action will prepare you to withstand future tests. Does this sound a little backward or unreasonable? It is just the way God planned it. He told Paul in 2 Corinthians 12:9 (NKJV), "My grace is sufficient for you, for My strength is made perfect in weakness." He's made for the tough things in life when we execute our faith in such a manner that we get out of the way with our thoughts, feelings, and actions and let Him be "I Am."

This is counter-cultural in every way but remember Heaven is upside down compared to the world (Acts 17:6 NKJV). Certain things that are permissible on earth are not present in Heaven. Since we are eternity bound, we need to make the choices that will help us get more familiar and comfortable with the behavior that is common in Heaven. We want to be able to step right in line upon arrival, already being accustomed to knowing how to think, feel, and act. We are given opportunities to bring Heaven on earth through our deportment and obedience. This is one of the greatest rewards as a child of God. We have a personal stake in changing the experiences people encounter. The Holy Spirit facilitates our success in this process. The characteristic of self-control is one of the biggest players in helping this occur consistently. Believers are urged to humble themselves and reflect on how bearing self-control has the potential to alter an outcome. It can change people's character, transform lives, and stir up curiosity about the source of such discipline. Witnessing the anointing power transferred from The Holy Spirit to the believer is evidence of the gains experienced when surrendering.

A wonderful illustration of exhibiting self-control when other actions were permissible and possibly warranted is the decision David made when faced with the opportunity to kill King Saul. David cut a piece of Saul's robe and could have easily killed him during this encounter. When David responded to his men as to why he did not kill Saul, he said that the Lord forbid that he should do such a thing to his master, the Lord's anointed. David forbade his men to harm Saul. (1 Samuel 24: 6-7 NKJV) We know that Saul hated David and had been hunting him down for some time. The average person would have been seen as justified in attacking and killing Saul. This is according to society's rules. David was clearly abiding by God's rules. When your actions are based on what God desires and not what man expects, you can exercise a good portion of self-control. Pastor Mike Todd of Transformation Church described self-control as choosing against "you" every day. We have to go against what is natural, desired, sought after to let The Holy Spirit control the man and not sin.

Many of us want to secure our spot in the fame line showing how determined, strong, and in charge we are. How we constantly use all of our brainpower to figure out the solutions and have shut out any interference trying to take the stage with us. It's got to be us alone for it to count. God longs for your willingness to let go and let God. He wants to know that your faith is going to help you commit to doing only what The Holy Spirit is directing in conquering the gigantic challenge facing you presently. The world says, "all hands on deck." God says, "my grace is sufficient. My strength is made perfect in your weakness" 2 Corinthians 12:9 KJV. It is a tug of war between behaving as you've always done, led by your own thoughts, and giving The Holy Spirit freedom to determine your responses or actions. There have been times you felt you had to show off and show out — at least that is what your spirit was shouting.

It is The Holy Spirit that is made for the battle, not your spirit. He is striving to guide your thoughts, actions, and feelings. This could be a big dilemma unless you take a stroll down memory lane and see all the other situations that worked out when you took your hands off the wheel. You relaxed and prepared to take instructions from The Holy Spirit. The times when you gladly received guidance and followed the instructions, there was success. The load got a bit lighter. For the moment, joy was multiplied. You weren't even tired. However, when disobedience reigned in the situation, there was a heaviness. The world did not feel lighter but rather heavily laden with cares. Hope was nowhere to be found, and you were struggling.

As a believer, you have the privilege and tools to choose in a manner that will further God's purpose on earth. We are God's workmanship, created for the work of His glory. Availing oneself for the use of the Divine Creator is worth breaking the ties of control and allowing oneself to be led freely to the execution of God's will. Once again, you are a chosen one to be used. Pride in the fact that you were selected by the Almighty will hopefully be sufficient. This can propel you to the point where you can contain your ego and embrace the wisdom of The Holy Spirit. God will be doing the heavy lifting on your behalf. Release so you can stand tall in the midst of the struggle. He's in control.

Fruitful Yield: Self-Control

Scripture to Read:

Look to yourselves, that we lose not those things which we have wrought, but that we receive a full reward (2 John 8 KJV).

Questions to Answer:

What will be your yield of self-control today?

Did you see self-control displayed today, and if so, how?

Thought to Ponder:

God made you with the power to determine the right choice. Let Him prove it to you.

Chapter XVI

The Blessing of Bearing (Your Inheritance)

●────────●────────●

"But the fruit of the Spirit is Love, Joy, Peace, Patience, Kindness, Goodness, Faith, Gentleness, and Self-Control"
(Galatians 5:22-23 ESV)

Well, we have been together exploring God's plan and how He perfected a way for all believers to engage in this plan and come out triumphant. Triumphant denotes victorious, winning a battle, jubilant in celebrating a conquest. This is the exact condition God wants His children to experience as they work through His plan for fruitfulness and godly living.

God's mission is for believers to create an abundant life through knowing His love, building a trusting and obedient relationship with The Holy Spirit and generating curiosity that leads others to seek God.

Now God does all this out of His love for us. The love of God is the greatest thing we can experience. What's so amazing is that most believers — and certainly unbelievers — don't come close to comprehending the magnitude and vastness of God's love, and how can we? He is everything that ever existed wrapped up into one being with three natures. He is God the Father, God the Son, who is Jesus Christ, and God The Holy Spirit. The fact that He has placed The Holy Spirit in us should let us know that He wants us to know that His love is extraordinary, available and constant.

God always has His eyes on His children. When believers are aware of this fact, it may encourage them to love, know and serve Him with their full capacity. This kind of awareness leads to genuine obedience to His commands and precepts.

By obeying God's command to man to be fruitful and multiply, we can create abundant living, which is part of His purpose for us. If we had to rely on our human abilities to foster transformation, the results would be pretty meager — with limited duration. However, we are created by a loving and all-powerful God. Believers have the assurance they possess the wherewithal to create lasting life-altering outcomes. The ones capable of producing abundance and righteousness. It is the presence of The Holy Spirit that makes this possible.

The Holy Spirit is the driver and knows the final destination and all the stops, detours, and crashes along the way. When the believer releases control and obeys The Holy Spirit, the consequences are aligned with God's purpose and have an eternal impact.

The Holy Spirit provides knowledge, wisdom, gifts, and power to the believer. He is also available to prompt and direct the believer in displaying the traits of Jesus — the fruit of the Spirit. This fruit is love, joy, peace, patience, kindness, goodness, faith, gentleness, and temperance. Remember, this is actually one fruit with nine characteristics associated with it. These traits were demonstrated routinely in Jesus' demeanor and heart during His time on earth. His sole purpose was to please God the Father, and His behavior did just that. This is why it is so important for the believer to accept The Holy Spirit's help in receiving and demonstrating these traits. The Holy Spirit is the Spirit of God and the Comforter, which Jesus promised would replace Him on earth. The Comforter helps, directs, and loves the believers through every moment of their journey on earth, preparing them for eternity with The Father. In this capacity, The Holy Spirit uses the fruit of the Spirit. A godly example is presented when such character is shown.

God expects such from His children, and He has provided the best person to facilitate such behavior from believers. To meet such expectations, our faith level has to continually grow.

Faith in God is needed when fully accepting The Holy Spirit, His attributes, and His power. The believer's faith goes on a journey of transformation in order to weather the situations and circumstances that will emerge throughout this human journey. Faith building is essential for the believer to arrive at the destination specifically created by God. As is written in the Bible, "without faith, it is impossible to please God" Hebrews 11:6 NKJV. Our life as a believer should focus on pleasing and glorifying God. A Father who gave His most precious possession to offer us eternal life. As a means to support the continuous transformation of our faith, there are actions or practices necessary to secure this movement of our faith.

These practices include prayer, daily Bible reading, meditating on the Word of God, and fellowshipping with other believers, to name a few. Now creating a pattern that may consistently include these actions is not easy. We all have many distractions in our lives that can quickly reroute our attention and priorities. God knew it would sometimes be a struggle to achieve regular adherence to these tested methods. This is why God made sure we did not have to only depend on our own strength and might to achieve something. He provided The Holy Spirit to every believer, dwelling inside to guide, protect, and reinforce. Earlier I shared how letting go of these practices led me to unwanted consequences -too numerous to mention. The most significant outcomes were the times my faith seemed to diminish.

Decreasing faith in God and His power can sidetrack a believer. Not only can it delay or deny reaching the goal God has identified for you, but the reality that one has allowed his faith to wean can affect mental health and the joy experienced. Beliefs of inadequacy, disobedience, and failure can set in and determine thoughts and affect feelings and actions. This can lead to behavior that is not representative of God or of the person. Many may fall into despair or depression when such shifts occur. Seasons such as these have appeared throughout my adult life. When I fully grasped that such seasons were not part of God's plan and that I had the power within me, The Holy Spirit, to build faith that could see me through, I committed to trying to make those practices sacred in my life. Now don't think I haven't slipped or been inconsistent. I have. But when that happens, The Holy Spirit is there to remind me of His function in my life. I have to have the right attitude and atmosphere to recognize His urging and commit to obeying whatever He is offering. He gives me the power to reconnect with these practices. Then I can strive again to live a life pleasing God.

The fruit of the Spirit — love, peace, joy, patience, kindness, goodness, faith, gentleness, and self-control — is ignited in me by The Holy Spirit. When my faith is built up and my practices are in place, I can readily follow the prompting of The Holy Spirit to receive these characteristics from Him and infuse them in my behavior. Notice that I said when. Remember, I just shared that I get off track frequently. I have to steady my mind, spirit, body, and surroundings to act on the awareness of The Holy Spirit's prompting. With His help, I can influence and change the atmosphere of my environment. The fruit of the Spirit reflects a portrait of how humanity was created to behave towards each other. People can react in positive ways when encountered by a believer yielding the fruit of the Spirit. The Holy Spirit is able to influence such reactions. He knows what is needed in every situation. When the believer acts in accordance with the direction of The Holy Spirit, the believer can produce exactly what is required to bring about an outcome that pleases God.

During the section of the book that highlighted each characteristic of the fruit of the Spirit, I shared the meanings of the characteristics, importance, and value of them and examples of how employing these characteristics brought about identifiable changes in the situations. Some examples were traditional stories associated with certain traits, and some might have been new to you. As you strengthen your relationship with The Holy Spirit and develop obedience, it may become more obvious that all the traits are powerful and effective in any situation. This is probably why God provided believers with The Holy Spirit to direct appropriate responses.

We know we will face circumstances that seem impossible. However, we can stand firm in our belief and knowledge that we are not alone. The Holy Spirit is ready, willing, and super able to lead us to a fruitful life. Once we accept that we can do nothing without God's permission and power, The Holy Spirit's help, and our acceptance of this protective and loving gift, we can start to enjoy the journey of truly building and owning the life God planned for us — fruitful and abundant.

Some of the quotes from throughout the book which hopefully reinforce a healthy reliance on God's plan, The Holy Spirit's purpose, and the believer's position are shared again below:

"Peace: not the absence of trouble but the tenacity to stay still in the midst of trouble."

"One of the most endearing gestures that we can bestow on another person is to be patient with them."

"The best time to go deep is when you are free from enormous pressure."

"My understanding doesn't produce truth."

As a believer, had I not experienced transformation in how I see The Holy Spirit and His place in my life, I would not know how much God delights in keeping me and working through me. He feels the same way towards all His children.

The Holy Spirit brings to my mind things long forgotten but needed in order for me to stay on assignment. He fills me with knowledge, wisdom, and strength for the race, no matter how many mistakes lined my path. There were many. During times I refused to hear The Holy Spirit, much less act on His guidance, He never left my side.

The dark places I strayed He was there. There were times when I couldn't join Him in prayer or praise, but He prayed for me and afterward struck up praise. All because He knew the work God created me to do, and He knew that I was not fulfilling the charge, but I could with Him. I needed to do my part.

The Holy Spirit's persistence is something to study and emulate. He is always perfect in His execution of helping us bear the fruit in the right season, promoting a righteous and lasting legacy. There will never be a season where the believer is not called, wanted, nudged to finish the work God wants done. God is depending on our love and obedience to make whatever adjustments are required to do His will. This determination is because of the fidelity, something greater than ourselves, involved in our spiritual walk. We are dealing with things that our minds cannot comprehend. Our minds are insufficient to understand the intricacies of God's creation and how the unity of it all will unfold.

Maintaining an intimate connection with and obedience to The Holy Spirit comes from the believer's devotion to doing the necessary work. The process of fertilizing the field and deep rooting is part of the strategy to build perseverance and discipline. The practices of prayer, reading the Bible, spending time with God, meditating on His Word, and spending time with other believers serve to assist the believer's heart in becoming more receptive and fertile. God reveals Himself and His plan through these activities.

The power inherent in these activities builds the believer's trust in God and acceptance of The Holy Spirit's role. The Holy Spirit does the heavy lifting. With the believer's commitment to living a life pleasing to God, The Holy Spirit is in every situation, providing instruction, direction, and counsel. The godly choice is always available to the believer. The practices shared in the Fertilizing the field section include prayer, reading the Bible, spending time with God, meditating on His Word, and fellowshipping with other believers. They can increase the probability that choices that please God may take priority over those that provide personal satisfaction.

It is the habit of deep rooting, protecting the spiritual practices so that they become entrenched in the believer, which can sustain the believer's commitment. This protection is a progressive and continual process. The best time to go deep is when you are free from enormous pressure. Making these practices part of your daily habit is key. God and The Holy Spirit can use an open and sensitive heart for their work in the believer. This openness and sensitivity develop through spiritual practices. These activities help the believer to be receptive towards the prompting of The Holy Spirit. Prayer, reading the Bible, spending time with God, meditating on His Word, and spending time with other believers are high-value activities. They are susceptible to attacks from satan and worldly distractions. They require the believer to shield themselves. Protecting the influence of The Holy Spirit in the life of the believer is paramount.

Knowing God and making Him known, it's a big assignment. The believer is lost without help. With The Holy Spirit's indwelling, there should be no fear of having to do anything alone. Our love for God should compel us to work towards doing whatever is necessary to make Him visible in the world. We always have The Holy Spirit to direct and join us in all of our endeavors. We are equipped for this journey through God's grace, mercy, and favor. His grace — God giving us what we don't deserve — allows us to continue to grow to maturity when we willingly respond to The Holy Spirit's petition. With man, the limits of willingness to help would probably be reached, and the attempts dismissed after countless tries. God is not man. He delights in showing mercy. When He shows us mercy, He withholds from us, what we do deserve. He permits The Holy Spirit to guide, not condemn, producing better outcomes. Finally, He rewards the obedience of His children with His favor. Favor in this moment is God's gift to us, allowing success in accomplishments that are seemingly impossible for humans. One of the most spectacular traits of God is His faithfulness. He is always faithful to His children, even when we are not faithful to Him. So, don't conclude your journey thinking God's rewards are only for the believers who are always in His will. He still has enough grace, mercy and favor for us at all times.

There is no action you take for God that is not created to share His glory with those involved in the situation. When the fruit of the Spirit is exhibited through the believer's thoughts, feelings, and actions, it is the light illuminating conditions, bringing clarity and understanding. When a believer routinely provides this healthy type of response, it can give others an opportunity to acquire curiosity about why and how this response is possible. An opening can be created to share more about God. That is the ultimate goal of our assignment.

God does His part. He creates us out of His love. He saves us through the sacrifice of His son, Jesus. He gives us The Holy Spirit to permanently dwell in us. He shows us the beauty of eternal life. He ensures we can make the right choices, those leading to conduct which pleases Him.

The believer's part in sustaining God's legacy is through sharing the gospel and drawing others towards Him. There is a persuasive argument made with the demonstration of the fruit of the Spirit in the life of the believer. The power and influence of God's love, The Holy Spirit's role, and the impact of the fruit of the Spirit produce perseverance for the journey. God planned it this way. Commit to His plan, honor Him, and see the fruit of your faith.

The demonstration of our faith offers a legacy for generations to come. The believer is changing due to the application of the fruit of the Spirit, but the environment is also susceptible to change. The believer's acceptance as an agent of such change pleases God. Helping others see the grace of God through interactions with one exhibiting godly- traits can have a profound impact. There are times when a fellow believer may need a reminder of the power within. Also, as children of God, this is what we do for family. We are all responsible for the positive spiritual development of our brothers and sisters. Fortunately, each of us possesses the means for authentic and influential engagement — the fruit of the Spirit-led by the guiding of The Holy Spirit.

Let believers show the world the best that God offers to achieve true fruitfulness. The believer operates best when synced with the movement of The Holy Spirit. Do not doubt or fear. As a believer, you are chosen, worthy, and capable of this important assignment in Kingdom building. With The Holy Spirit in you using the fruit of the Spirit, you have the ability to change the trajectory and create a legacy honoring God and His children.

Please do yourself and me a big favor. Take some time to digest what you have experienced during our journey through this book. Let it resonate and be open to allowing The Holy Spirit to move you further on the path. Whether you are actively embracing your relationship with The Holy Spirit or just know of Him as part of the Trinity, this book is meant to move you further along your journey with God. Spend some time doing the activities found in the "Fruitful Yield" sections of the chapters covering each trait. Let them serve as a guide to heighten your awareness of the presence and power of the fruit of the Spirit in your life, made available by The Holy Spirit.

Enjoy your position in God and with God. He created a very special part in His plan for you. Through faith to believe God is who He says He is and that He gave the greatest sacrifice, giving up His only son, you can know, encounter, and benefit from all of Him. This is the door that leads to the degree of fruitful living God wants for you. Grow towards strengthening your belief, expanding your faith, and accepting the gift of The Holy Spirit wholeheartedly. This is the true way to achieve God's bounty for you — a fruitful life.

www.ingramcontent.com/pod-product-compliance
Lightning Source LLC
Chambersburg PA
CBHW070202100426
42743CB00013B/3017